"WHY DON'T YOU LIKE ME?"

UNCONSCIOUS BIAS AND THE
CHANGING MOSAIC OF OUR NATION

MITCHELL L. SPRINGER

"Why Don't You Like Me?"
Unconscious Bias and the Changing Mosaic of Our Nation

ISBN: 978-1-946533-87-6 eBook
978-1-946533-88-3 Hardback
978-1-946533-89-0 Paperback
Library of Congress Control Number: 2020904175

DISCLAIMER

The views and opinions expressed in this book are those of the author. Examples of analysis performed within this book are only examples and should not be utilized in real-world analytic products or processes as they are based solely on limited and current date open-source information. This information is provided and sold with the knowledge that the publisher and author do not offer any legal or other professional advice. In the case of a need for any such expertise, consult with the appropriate professional. This book does not contain all information available on the subject. This book has not been created to be specific to any individual's or organization's situation or needs. Although the author and publisher have made every effort to ensure that the information in this book was correct at press time, the author and publisher do not assume and hereby disclaim any liability to any party for any loss, damage, or disruption caused by errors or omissions, whether such errors or omissions result from negligence, accident, or any other cause. The information contained within this book is provided for informational purposes only and should not be construed as legal advice on any matter. Recipients of information contained herein should not act upon this information without seeking professional counsel.

For permission to reprint portions of this content or for bulk purchases, contact the author at mlspring@purdue.edu

Published by Niche Pressworks; http://NichePressworks.com

With Sincere Gratitude

"Why am I here?" Ever find yourself asking this? "What is my purpose?" On May 8, 2015, I was told I had 12-14 months to live, and then, I would have simply been watching TV or walking outside, and I would have died instantly from a massive 90% blockage in my left coronary artery (a.k.a. The Widow Maker).

As I was being prepped for surgery, the most sobering moment of my life was when they asked if I wanted to see a priest. I suspected for last rites, telling me there was a possibility I could die during the procedure. Somehow, I knew this was not my time. I had been groomed from my life's beginning to do something. To do more and be more. I just didn't know what 'more' was.

I am so thankful for the positive and negative things that have happened in my life. I am thankful for the many people I have come to know and learn from and the opportunities I have had in my career in the defense industry, as well as my second career in higher education.

I appreciate the skills and abilities I have been afforded, and I am thankful for the childhood I experienced living without resources. It taught me things I would not have learned otherwise.

Perhaps most importantly, I am thankful for my family and especially my wife. It was my wife who saved me. As a medical provider for a heart and lung center, she was the lone voice demanding I have an angiogram performed. She identified the real threat. She saved my life.

No book is written alone. Special thanks to my good friend and publisher Nicole and her amazing team of professionals, Kim and Kathie. Wow! Such a knowledgeable group.

With my most sincere gratitude, I say "Thank You" to all those who have made my life's journey such an amazing experience. I am grateful to have been given this life—all of the good and all of the bad.

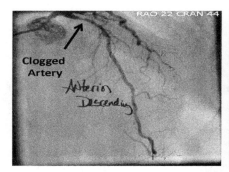 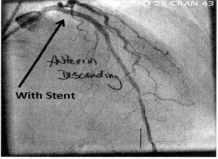

LEFT CORONARY ARTERY (WITH 90% BLOCKAGE)

Contents

AND THE STORY BEGINS...

What is This Book About?

Over a holiday break, two of my family members were putting together a puzzle with hundreds of pieces. They kept looking back at the picture on the box to see how the pieces fit together. Without that bigger perspective, they would have struggled to see the whole from the pieces.

This book is a collection of seemingly unrelated topics, but when they're brought together under a common lens, they reflect a "Wow! I didn't see that coming!" response.

When these independent fragments are put together—like puzzle pieces—the result is a new reimagined perspective. In this case, why we may not feel at ease with what we are experiencing in today's world.

"Why Don't You Like Me?" is not about me. 'Me' is all of us. The questions become: why don't others like us? Why don't we like them?

The premise for this discussion is in understanding who we are and why others may cause us to feel uneasy, fearful, or any similarly negative responses.

Our world is changing.

> *Our unconscious biases will have magnified opportunity to manifest in behaviors that will be better, or, divisively worse.*

Whether our behaviors are magnified as good or bad will depend on our awareness and understanding of what is happening and why.

I have spent my professional life heightening awareness of the behaviors of unconscious bias toward those who are looked upon differently because of who they are. Our society can only be as good as its members. Through greater understanding of ourselves and others, we can be better. We can help shape a better nation and world.

This book reflects on the changing face of our country. It addresses three significant shifts happening right now and as far into the future as we can see. The book also reviews topics tightly coupled to these three major shifts, namely: (1) the changing racial and ethnic face of our nation, (2) the shortage of younger individuals to backfill our society, and (3) the rapid aging of massive numbers within our society.

> *In the end, "Why Don't You Like Me?" addresses how we can be our better selves.*

I am not out to change anyone's mind on whether they like or dislike the societal changes currently underway. I have long since learned I cannot do this. I am simply here to heighten awareness of these many changes already happening. To bring to the forefront that which exists as the undercurrent of societal change. Perhaps, in doing so, each of us may think about how our thoughts are manifested into behaviors, and more importantly, why. Why don't we like someone?

Why Won't You Talk to Me?

Our city began desegregation shortly after my family moved from the south side of town to a mobile home park on the north side. The schools bussed kids from the old neighborhood, and it was a violent time. Fights broke out every day, and the police walked our hallways.

A female friend of mine was one of those bussed to my new school. We were in several classes together and talked and laughed together frequently. We sat together at lunch, and we enjoyed each other's company. She was more than my friend.

Well into the academic year, she came into school one day from having just gotten off the bus. I saw her walking in the hall and yelled out to her to stop. She kept walking. I figured she didn't hear me through the hustle and bustle of the hall chatter. I yelled again as I got closer to her. Still, no response. Finally, I got right next to her, placed my hand on her back, and said, "Hey, wait for me."

She looked around me to the stairwell, then at me. She had tears in her eyes when she told me, "I can't talk to you anymore." I detected the hurt and asked why not. She said, "I can't. You have to go. I can't talk to you anymore." My stomach sank; I felt heartbroken. I stopped her. "Why not?" She looked again at the stairwell. "I am not allowed to."

I looked over my shoulder and could see three males our age who rode the bus with her. They were staring at us. I asked, "Because of them?" She nodded and moved down the hall. I was confused, angry, and just plain ticked off. My keenly honed old neighborhood demeanor kicked in. I moved quickly to the stairs to physically address the three who were standing there. I learned how to fight in the old neighborhood, had been punched in the face, had my nose broken three times, and wasn't afraid of conflict. They scattered when they saw me coming. I knew this would continue.

This crushed me. After all, I had lived in the south part of town and was a member of that community. I'd experienced it, understood it, and felt it. My friends were as multi-cultural and multi-racial as any group could be. I had no preconceived prejudices against any race or culture, even though there were numerous people I disliked. The three from the stairwell, for example. I felt like I had when people took advantage of us for being poor. It wasn't right. I felt angry, sad, helpless, and angry again.

It didn't take long for confrontations to occur. I left during class to go to the restroom, and in came the three guys from the stairwell. Fights in the bathrooms were a common occurrence during this time, so I knew very well what was about to happen. And to be honest, I wanted it to happen.

The name-calling began. They weren't short of names for me, making comments of all kinds about my mother and my anatomical parts.

I immediately moved to swear words. I pushed myself into the biggest of the three, cursing and swearing like all you-know-what was about to break loose. They all seemed surprised by this move, and two of them backed away. The biggest, now pushed against the wall, seemed a little shell shocked. I stopped, realizing they didn't want to fight. I yelled a few choice words and stalked out.

In the end, they were like me; scared kids caught up in something new. They were trying to fit in. I guess I really didn't want to fight either. I just wanted my friend back.

Ironically, that guy and I became friends. I never got a chance to rekindle my friendship with my female friend, however.

In looking back, those were difficult, turbulent times. Things were changing, and we—as youths—didn't understand a lot of what was going on. Why couldn't we all be friends? Why couldn't we all hang around together? Why did I lower myself to swearing, fighting, and all the in-your-face stuff? And why couldn't I still be friends with my female friend? Was it really just because we were of different races?

I am not proud of the person I was as a child. I could have been better. In looking back, I **should** have been better. In many regards, my culture formed me. I became what I had to be to survive. I was skinny, disheveled, and lacked direction. Fortunately, 'childhood me' changed for the better when I went to work for the defense industry.

The Worst Part of Being Poor is Not Knowing How Not to Be Poor

When I look back on my childhood, remembering the simple things makes me smile. I remember from my earliest years looking forward to the Christmas holidays. For me, this began with autumn and Halloween. I couldn't wait for *It's the Great Pumpkin, Charlie Brown* to come on television. It was the kick-off of fall for me.

I had *Charlie Brown,* the smell of burning leaves, and the crispness that comes with the autumn. There was football in sweatshirts and raking leaves just to run and leap into them. These are my memories of my childhood during this season.

Later in the year, my mother would take me downtown to see the big Christmas tree in the town square. It stood way up on top of the primary intersection where cars drove under it. To me, it seemed to stand hundreds of feet in the air.

We would walk past the old Wolf & Dessauer Department Store. There, in the windows stretching for blocks, were the most beautiful Christmas decorations. I saw animated mechanical figures, and trains moved for blocks through the store's front windows. I looked up into the black night sky as snow fell, realizing there was something bigger than me. Something deep and rich in meaning. I didn't want the feeling to end.

From this description, you'd think I led a different life, not one entrenched in poverty. Our living room ceiling had holes open to the sky, and when it rained, my mother put pots and pans on the floor to collect the water as it drip, drip, dripped into our living space.

The house we rented had big oak trees in the backyard whose roots had long since clogged our sewer pipes. We put buckets under our sinks to collect the water and then dump it out as far away from the house as we could carry it.

We didn't have enough fuel oil to keep us warm, and Mom piled nearly all my clothes on me at night, so I wouldn't get cold.

I can remember often going to bed hungry. I know how the stomach pangs of hunger slowly dissipate and how headaches and lightheadedness follow.

But the memories I choose to remember most often are the good ones.

My mom and I would go to the quickie mart down the block from where we lived. Sometimes we wouldn't have enough money for a loaf of bread, milk, or one of the other essentials. Mom would make a game of our scanning the parking lot for whatever change we might find.

I would yell out, "I found a penny!" She'd say, "I found another penny!" On rare occasions, we might find a nickel or dime. What a great discovery that was! Together we would laugh and quickly add up how much we had collectively. I learned early on not to ask for anything while in the store. All it took was seeing Mom tear up and say, "No, we don't have the money."

For many, cutting to the core of having less is a deep-seated desire to break free.

> *Perhaps the worst part of being poor is not knowing how not to be poor. Not knowing how to get out.*

No education. No money. Minimal, low-paying opportunities. It all translates to 'going without.' When you are poor, it doesn't go away. It's there every day, day in, and day out. You don't just miss out on material possessions. Being poor cheats you out of necessities. It causes extreme stress and all the physical and mental ailments that go along with it.

Poverty is a stigma, and many people treat it as a social disease. People looked at us differently. They treated us differently. Even under today's discrimination laws, poverty is not a protected class.

On the positive side, having less provided me with internal motivators. It created independence, strategic thinking, and perhaps most important, a burning desire to be more. I would not be the person I am today if it were not for my childhood experiences.

We Control Whether it is the Best or the Worst of Giving Forward

Who am I to write a book on diversity, equity, and inclusion? After all, I fit into most privileged classes. I am non-Hispanic White (Caucasian) unless you go back three generations. Here you find my great-great-grandmother, who was African American.

But, if you go back 300,000 years, we all evolved from African descent. It was only in these last 100,000 years we began to spread through most of modern-day Europe, Asia, and the rest of the world. Sort of makes you wonder why we have a problem with race, doesn't it, given we all started from the same place?

I am a male heterosexual, and I have been Protestant, Catholic, Lutheran, Methodist, and then Catholic again. (I was granted an annulment). I have financial resources and education. I fit into nearly every definition of 'privileged' (someone who enjoys an exclusive right or treatment).

What in the world would I know of the struggles of life? I hope my experiences, sprinkled throughout this book, help provide my credentials. I cannot speak to every discriminating characteristic, but I can speak to a few. Through this, I hope others can personalize and internalize them from their own.

> *We each must see and feel discrimination through the lens of our lives. It is emotions over memories that emblazon the event and cause its internalization.*

When we face discrimination, we understand the attendant emotions, anxieties, anger, and fears. The richness and vividness of the experiences bring the defining characteristics to life. The significance of the lessons ensures we don't forget.

We all have experiences, positive and negative. All we can ever ask of another is they stop for a moment to reflect on how their actions and behaviors might impact those around us. How our words, actions, and non-actions alike, affect the subsequent actions and non-actions of those we have affected.

> *We control whether it is the best or the worst of giving forward.*

PART 1: THREE MAJOR TECTONIC CHANGES SHAPING OUR NATION

If you have watched TV over the last few years, you will notice something different. You will see more diversity among broadcasters, news reporters, and TV personalities. You will see more TV commercials with mixed couples of varying racial and ethnic origins. Series, which once marginally had non-white actors, now have combinations of races and ethnicities.

> *Statisticians expect the U.S. population to become significantly more racially and ethnically diverse, grow more slowly, and age (gray) considerably.*

It is not uncommon to see mixed-race or mixed-ethnic marriages or co-habitations, gay and lesbian open expressions, and more.

What about those Medicare and other old-age-related commercials? Or medicine-related commercials? Isn't it interesting there are so many new commercials for adult diapers or erectile dysfunction?

TV has changed. It's beginning to reflect the changing face of our nation, the actual makeup of our mosaic society.

At this writing, this book is going to press during the early outbreak of COVID-19. While the full implications of this pandemic are yet to be understood, we can be certain there will be lasting implications on each of the many age demographic groups in our society. The data presented in this book reflects that which leads up to this pandemic. It will take years to determine how this pandemic will change or alter that which we currently have actual data for.

CHAPTER 1

The Basis for the Story is the Changing U.S. Demographics

How far must we search to find something we do not like about another person's race, ethnicity, or other defining characteristics? What human emotions enter into this equation? Anger, jealousy, envy, fear?

> *If you have theoretical and/or practical experience in management, you can likely manage what you do not understand. However, you cannot lead it.*

This statement, in a modified form, was first put forth by Myron Tribus in 1996. We cannot lead a diverse group of people if we do not understand them. It is true in business and a nation. This book heightens awareness about the changing nature of American demographics and the social, political, and economic undertones of our changing face.

*Once I saw this guy on a bridge about to jump. I said, "Don't do it!" He said, "Nobody loves me." I said, "God loves you. Do you believe in God?" He said, "Yes." I said, "Are you a Christian or a Jew?" He said, "A Christian." I said, "**Me, too!**"*

*"Protestant or Catholic?" He said, "Protestant." I said, "**Me, too!**"*

*"What franchise?" He said, "Baptist." I said, "**Me, too!**"*

*"Northern Baptist or Southern Baptist?" He said, "Northern Baptist." I said, "**Me, too!**"*

*"Northern Conservative Baptist or Northern Liberal Baptist?" He said, "Northern Conservative Baptist." I said, "**Me, too!**"*

*"Northern Conservative Baptist Great Lakes Region, or Northern Conservative Baptist Eastern Region?" He said, "Northern Conservative Baptist Great Lakes Region." I said, "**Me, too!**"*

"Northern Conservative Baptist Great Lakes Region Council of 1879, or Northern Conservative Baptist Great Lakes Region Council of 1912?" He said, "Northern Conservative Baptist Great Lakes Region Council of 1912."

I said, "Die, heretic!" And I pushed him over. —EMO PHILIPS

The populous of our country is undergoing a transformation, the likes of which have never before been experienced in the United States of America. The demographic changes, which surfaced in the literature and became more pronounced just over a decade ago, are now on the verge of a tectonic shift. We feel their impact on every aspect of our lives, from TV to higher education and from politics to our homes and personal lives.

Three major events will take place over the upcoming decade. Although each is significant by itself, they have generally gone unnoticed. Together, they are transformative and paint an ever-changing face of our United States.

The first of these changes is the racial and ethnic composition of our nation. This transition represents the new 'minority-majority' of America (or the 'majority-minority') where the non-Hispanic White population becomes the minority overall for the first time in U.S. history.

The second of the three changes is a shortfall of bench strength due to the crossover where the number of people 65+ years of age is greater than the youths under the age of 18. In other words, there is a shortage of young people to replace an aging generation.

The impact of this transition is reflected in the number of working-age individuals compared to those not working. When youth dependency (those under the age of 18) is added to the old-aged dependency (government term), the net effect is a total dependency where there are two dependents for every three working-age adults.

The third and final significant change is the 'graying' of America. The last of the baby boomers (born between 1946 and 1964) will turn 65 years of age by December 31, 2029. This is particularly significant because of the financial impacts on social services and safety nets currently supporting our aging population.

These three primary drivers of demographic change are already being felt in our businesses, educational institutions, lives, and homes.

CHAPTER 2

Our Growing Racial and Ethnic Diversities

Our country is aging and growing more slowly. This is especially true for non-Hispanic Whites. The fastest-growing groups for the next four decades are two or more races (+197%), Asians (+101%), and Hispanics (+93%)[1]. Non-Hispanic Whites is the only group expected to decline (a drop of over 19 million people). This negative 9.6% growth reflects the general aging of this population, coupled with its decreasing fertility rates.

According to projections, while Non-Hispanic Whites (Caucasians) remain the single largest cohort, by 2045, they will no longer be the majority in the U.S.

---

1   Vespa, J., Armstrong, D., and Medina, L. (2018). Demographic Turning Points for the United States: Population Projections for 2020 to 2060. Current population Reports, P25-1144, U.S. Census Bureau, Washington, DC. P. 7

THE NEW MINORITY-MAJORITY IN 2020

As with any country, the youth of the U.S. is the bench strength of the nation. These members backfill for the aging and are the primary workers for sustaining age-related social programs. They are the strength of the working class and hold the keys to our innovation. This group must be sufficiently educated and capable of sustaining an ongoing enterprise (or, in this case, a country).

In the year 2020, less than one-half of the children under 18 years of age will be Caucasian (thus, a minority). This crossover comes with a new term: either 'the new minority-majority' or 'the new majority-minority' (when referring to non-Hispanic Whites).

In the year 2020, under-18 Caucasians will represent 49.8% of the total youth. The combined minorities will exceed the non-Hispanic White population for the first time in U.S. history. By 2060, roughly two-thirds of the youths will be Non-Hispanic White. This trend is not expected to reverse since significantly higher growth of the combined minority groups continues to outpace this one.

The 116th Congress of the United States depicts this changing face of America. The House of Representatives, elected in 2016, has more women, women of color, openly LGBT members, and millennials serving than ever before, and nearly every member now holds a college degree.

This last point aligns with the idea of higher levels of education promoting a greater degree of acceptance and understanding. Topics or issues are not as likely to be seen as merely left or right, top or bottom, black or white. There are shades of gray.

FIGURE 1.1—116TH CONGRESS OF THE UNITED STATES OF AMERICA

INTERNATIONAL MIGRATION IS KEY TO U.S. POPULATION GROWTH

The natural-born U.S. populous is getting older and not having as many babies as in previous years. Who is going to pay taxes to support our aging nation? How do we find those to buy all that is required to continue our growth?

As we have done previously, we experience growth through immigration.

Projections show that, by 2028, the foreign-born percentage share in the U.S. will be higher than at any time since 1850 (15.2%, exceeding the previous high of 14.8%). The overall share should continue increasing since the natural-born group's fertility rate declines as it ages.

In 2030, the net natural-born increase to the population (due to natural-born U.S. citizens) will be roughly 1 million, while at the same time, the net international immigration increase will be roughly 1.1 million.

Through 2060, the net international migration increase will remain stable at 1.1 million, while the natural-born net will continue declining (due to a decreasing birthrate).

This overall decline in the natural-born population reflects an increasing populous at a decreasing rate of growth. That means there are fewer and fewer of the natural-born over time (or a decreasing birthrate).

As we have done in previous decades, allowing people into our country is crucial to our ongoing success as a nation.

MILLENNIALS USHER IN MINORITY-MAJORITY

Given the new minority-majority is here, it seems only appropriate that we learn more about who they are.

The millennials (Gen Y), span the years 1981 through 1996. They follow the veterans, baby boomers, and Gen Xers:

- **Veterans** (Traditionalist) 1922-1945; 52 million people; born before and during WW II
- **Baby Boomers** 1946-1964; 78.8 million people; after WW II; reared during a period of optimism, opportunity, and progress. Began turning 65 on January 1, 2011; aging to 65 years old at 10,000/day, through December 31, 2029.
- **Generation X** (Gen X) 1965-1980; 44 million people; came of age in the shadow of the boomers; children of veterans, older boomers, or younger siblings of younger boomers.
- **Generation Y** (Millennials) 1981-1996; 75.3 million people; children of younger boomers and known as the 'most loved' generation.

- **Generation Z** (Gen Z) 1997-2012; population yet to be defined; children of Gen X.

In 2015, the millennials (Gen Y) became the largest adult group, surpassing the baby boomers. In this same year, Gen Y surpassed Gen X as the most significant force in the U.S. labor market. In 2015, millennials made up 25% of the U.S., roughly 30% of voters, and nearly 40% of the workforce.

In 2018, millennials were 55.8% white and nearly 30% new minorities: Hispanic, Asian, and those identifying as two or more races. Millennials are more racially and ethnically diverse than previous cohorts. This fact will only be superseded by Gen Z.

A large percentage of the growth in minorities stems from the migration into the U.S. from Latin America and Asia. These immigrants are typically younger and have growing families.

Gen Z will define future diversity growth. In 2020, the underrepresented minority became the majority (if we consider children under the age of 18). One-third of Gen Z is, by definition, a minority.

From this perspective, the millennials ushered in the nation's future diversity. Gen Z follows, solidifying and defining the racial and ethnic trend line.

THE MILLENNIAL (GEN Y) VIEW OF DIVERSITY AND INCLUSIVITY

Given millennials and Gen Z are now the majority of our combined population and are representative of the new minority-majority, what do they think about diversity and inclusion? Do their views differ from previous generations?

The answer is, "Yes."

Deloitte University, in collaboration with the Billie Jean King Leadership Initiative, reported on an exhaustive study reflecting Gen Y views of diversity and inclusion.

In this study, Deloitte reported, "...millennials view inclusion as having a culture of connectedness that facilitates teaming, collaboration, and professional growth."[2]

A few of the key takeaways from this report include:

- When defining diversity, millennials are 35% more likely to focus on unique experiences, whereas 21% of non-millennials usually focus on representation.

- When asked about the business impact of diversity, millennials are 71% more likely to focus on teamwork compared with 28% of non-millennials, who are more likely to look at the fairness of opportunity.

- Eighty-three percent of millennials are actively engaged when they believe their organization fosters an inclusive culture. Only 60% are actively engaged when their organization does not foster an inclusive culture.

---

2   Smith, C., Turner, S. (2016). *The Radical Transformation of Diversity and Inclusion: The Millennial Influence*. Deloitte University, The Leadership Center for Inclusion. Downloaded from https://www2.deloitte.com/us/en/pages/about-deloitte/articles/radical-transformation-of-diversity-and-inclusion.html. P. 3

- Millennials believe programs aimed at diversity and inclusion should focus on improved business opportunities and outcomes as a result of the acceptance of cognitive diversity (individualism), collaboration, teamwork, and innovation.

Millennials strive to be inclusive, but differently from boomers and Gen-Xers, who focus on assimilating individuals of different races, genders, ethnicities, religions, and sexual orientations. This assimilation is referred to as moving from Point A to Point B. Millennials want to move from Point B to Point C, rather than focusing on previous definitions for diversity and inclusion.

With Point C, millennials are more concerned with the diversity of thoughts, ideas, and philosophies. They want to capitalize on these differences and solve business problems through collaboration.

By 2025, millennials will represent 75% of the total U.S. workforce. Since they change jobs approximately every two years, 75% of CEOs and executive-level leaders believe leveraging cognitive diversity is essential to ongoing organizational success.

Alternatively stated, millennials frame diversity as a means to a business outcome, which is in contrast to those prior generations viewing diversity through the lens of morality (the right thing to do), compliance, and equality.

Predecessors to the millennials most commonly define diversity as the representation of and fairness to all individuals and their various identifiers of gender, race, religion, ethnicity, and sexual orientation. This older group wants to ensure the mix on teams represents fairness (based on gender, race, religion, ethnicity, and sexual orientation).

However, millennials look past these identifiers to focus on the knowledge, experience, and unique insights individuals bring forth.

> *The blending of unique perspectives within a team—to combine different ideas and approaches to overcome challenges and achieve goals— is the definition of millennial diversity.*

Just as diversity is viewed from a continuing lens, so too is inclusion. Millennials define inclusion as having a culture of connectedness that facilitates teaming, collaboration, and professional growth. Inclusion positively affects major business outcomes. Previously, 'inclusion' was the acceptance or tolerance of historically named underrepresented minorities.

Prior generations to millennials view inclusion as the manner in which organizations ensure all employees are treated fairly and provide opportunities consistent with others within the organization. These prior perspectives frequently aligned with government regulation as it relates to equal employment laws.

Millennials and non-millennials offer differing perspectives on inclusion.

From a millennial perspective, inclusion is:

- Having an impact at all levels, open lines of communication, transparency, and strategic initiatives communicated to employees by executives.

- Being a part of the process, your opinion counts, and you're working with others to achieve a common goal. It is being accountable for your decisions.
- Coming together to accomplish a goal, interacting with other staff, and forming business relationships.

From an older, non-millennial perspective, inclusion is when everyone in the organization has equal opportunity to work and grow without any bias towards religion, race, or gender.

Millennials are 28% more likely to focus on business impact, 71% more likely to center on teamwork, and focus on a culture of connectedness 22% more. Older age groups look more often at fairness or opportunity (28%), equity (31%), integration (26%), and are 28% more likely to focus on acceptance or tolerance.

Moving from Point A to Point B recognizes most diversity and inclusion models (which have originated over the last 30+ years). These models include positive advancements around employee affinity programs, diversity councils, and minority training programs. These programs and initiatives have done more to advance our understanding of the value of diversity and inclusion. Millennials feel these programs and initiatives were useful, but are limited to one-dimensional characteristics of race, gender, ethnicity, and sexual orientation.

Cognitive diversity (and its resulting form of inclusion) is strongly related to innovation. Three-fourths of millennials believe their organization fosters greater innovation when an inclusive culture exists. Diversity and inclusion enhance creativity. Companies with high levels of innovation reflect the fastest growth of profits and generate ten times more shareholder value than slower incremental changes.

This is similar to the business case for diversity: business growth comes from innovation, innovation comes from a pool of ideas, and ideas come from people. All people.

CHAPTER 3

Our Shrinking Bench Strength— the Fewer, Newer, More Challenged Us

When we address the shrinking bench strength of our youth, we have to look at not only the declining birthrates but the subsequent dwindling number of high school graduates going to college. The follow-on discussion centers on what our colleges and universities are doing to bring more of those who would not otherwise go to college into those ranks. Are we already overeducated?

MY FIRST JOB OUT OF COLLEGE— EDUCATION ACTS AS A FORCE MULTIPLIER

I learned and matured so much during my first job out of college, all because of the military personnel I was in contact with on a daily basis. These individuals taught me about integrity, honesty, honor, loyalty, and being committed to something bigger than ourselves. I came to realize how they put themselves in harm's way every day so the rest of us could work, eat, go to movies, and sleep without fear of being killed, bombed, or captured.

This was all new to me. Stemming from my childhood, I was always thinking about making a buck. It was always about survival. I had no loyalties and no real friends. I didn't want friends and felt working alone was an easier and quicker way to get things done.

Designing some of the world's most sophisticated software and hardware systems for our fighting men and women of the U.S. Armed Forces was a great privilege for me. It is something I wear as a badge of honor.

I am proud of my opportunity to serve on teams with these men and women, and working with them made me want to be a better person. I grew from a disheveled kid into a professional.

This sentiment and a strong sense of commitment did not happen on day one. It resulted from a chance meeting with a major in the U.S. Army. He asked me, very early in my career, if I knew why I did what I did (as a software engineer, building military systems). I told him, "Yes. To make money."

With his vast knowledge, he showed me how I could be a better engineer and a better person.

"You will come to realize your job is about the greater good," he began, "to serve and support those who put their lives on the line. If you only do your job to make money, you will move from job to job. You may be good at it and even be proud of it. But you will **miss the satisfaction of doing it for someone else.** If you realize the greater reason for doing your job, you will take great pride in your work. You will want to do it better."

The major was right on so many fronts. Internalizing what we do creates a sense of ownership and pride. Then, it's no longer 'just a job.' It becomes a necessary, important part of the greater good. Internalizing the vision makes it personal.

I do a lot of research on the problems of today's college graduates dealing with rising college and health care costs as well as home and car expenses. Economists tell us it took roughly 27 years (from 1947 to 1973) for our standard of living to double, but it will take 268 years for it to double again. President George Bush commented on this, saying Gen-X will not have the same lifestyle their boomer parents experienced.

THE SHRINKING YOUTH POPULATION

In the U.S., a person's working phase is between the ages of 18 and 64. Those below the age of 18 are 'youth,' while those aged 65 and above are categorized as 'senior non-working.'

In the ideal scenario, youth backfill for the aging and become the workers ensuring the continuation of social programs (Social Security, Medicare, etc.).

In 2035—for the first time in U.S. history—the 65+ cohort is expected to outnumber the youth (under 18 years old).

The shift from a youth-dependent to an elderly-dependent population has significant implications. The combination of youth and old-age dependency is even more revealing. In the year 2020, the total dependency ratio (as a measure of the burden on the working-age group) is 64%. This means that, in 2020, there are two dependents for every three working-age adults. This ratio reflects slower growth, a declining fertility rate, and an aging demographic.

Retirement impacts this discussion. Current economic, political, and social events cause some of those eligible for full retirement (as defined by the U.S. Social Security Administration) to delay it. While there are significant previously-reported data points on this topic, the real impact—at this time—is uncertain. I mention it to heighten awareness and raise consciousness.

COHORT GROUP—GEN Z

Gen Z is the newest and youngest group on our radar screens. Since Gen Z roughly spans the years 1997-2012, its members are currently between the ages of 8 and 23.

> *Gen Z is by far the most racially and ethnically diverse of our population, and it is on track to becoming the largest generation in U.S. history.*

Who are the Gen Z members?

The year 2013 marked the crossover: more minority children were born than non-Hispanic White. By 2020, the minority-majority went from being under the age of one to under the age of 18. This indicates a rapid rate of change in the race and ethnicity of newborns.

This generation has had several good books written about it. Two, in particular, are solidly based on extensive and exhaustive surveys. They are *Gen Z Goes to College*[3] and *iGen*[4].

As Gen Z came on the scene, Pixar released the movie *Toy Story*, Michael Jordan returned to the NBA from retirement, *Titanic* was the most popular film, and gas was only $1.22 per gallon.

Perhaps cooler was the technology. Gen Z was the first to have one device for playing video games, making phone calls, listening to music, and computing. We baby boomers needed four devices to accommodate these functions. Does anyone else remember these items?

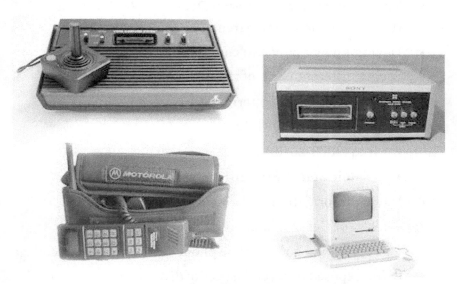

FIGURE 3.1—IMAGES OF TECHNOLOGY FROM PRIOR GENERATIONS (DOWNLOADED FROM GOOGLE IMAGES)

---

3   Seemiller, C. & Grace, M. (2016). *Generation Z Goes to College*. San Francisco, CA.: Jossey-Bass.
4   Twenge, J. (2017). *iGen*. New York, NY.: Simon and Schuster Inc.

Gen Zers are:

- The children of Gen X
- Those born between 1997 and 2012
- One-third of the U.S. population
- The most racially diverse group—Ever!

Major events define Gen Z, such as:

- The September 11, 2001, attacks on the United States. While they were too young to remember it, they have been aware of the continuing cultural implications.
- The economic crash between December 2007 and June 2009. It impacted Gen Zers' parents.
- Having known only two contrasting U.S. Presidents.
- Seeing different parts of the world at war:
  - ▸ The global war on terror (2001-present)
  - ▸ Afghanistan (2001-2014)
  - ▸ Iraq (2003-2010)
  - ▸ Islamic State (ISIS) (2014-present)
- Having information at their fingertips with:
  - ▸ 90% of Gen Z adults owning mobile phones.
  - ▸ 78% having had a mobile phone before arriving at college.
- Being exposed to several issues of diversity and social justice.

When you think of Gen Zers, characterize them as:

- Using technology to find solutions to problems.
- Having a strong work ethic similar to the boomers.
- Being responsible and resilient like their Gen X parents.

38

- Being technologically savvier than millennials (Gen Y).
- Describing themselves as loyal (85%), thoughtful (80%), compassionate (73%), open-minded (70%), and responsible (90%).

GEN Z STRESSORS

In looking at Gen Z stress and mental health issues, it appears the members are more stressed at their age than prior groups.

Sixty-eight percent of Gen Zers report feeling very or somewhat significantly stressed about our nation's future. Across generations and regarding mental health issues, Gen Zers were most likely to report problems (91%), least likely to say their mental health was either good or very good (45%), and most likely to have received treatment for their problems (37%).

Gen Z common stressors include personal issues, national matters, and gun violence.

Adult Gen Z members report feeling more stressed (than adults overall) about topics such as mass shootings, rising suicide rates, climate change, and global warming. They are also concerned about separating and deporting immigrant and migrant families, widespread sexual harassment, and assault reports.

Slightly more than 9 in 10 (91%) of Gen Zers between the ages of 18 and 21 say they have experienced at least one physical or emotional symptom due to stress in the past month, versus 74% of adults overall who say they have experienced at least one symptom.

When it comes to personal life stressors, work and money top the list for both Gen Z and adults overall. Health-related concerns and the economy follow.

On the economy, Gen Z reports slightly less stress (46%) than adults overall (48%). Youthfulness is the likely reason for economic concern. Work and money are typical pocketbook issues as Gen Zers move out of their parents' homes, buy or rent places to live, have children, and begin making purchases aligned to adult life phases.

Minority Gen Z typically reports stress more than their non-minority peers. For around four in ten of minority Gen Zers, personal debt (41%) and housing instability (40%) are significant sources of stress. Three in ten non-minority Gen Z members (30%) say the same about personal debt, and less than one quarter (24%) of non-minority Gen Zers cite housing instability. This disparity between minority Gen Z and their non-minority peers includes percentages reporting hunger as a significant source of stress.

Overall, individuals from each of the cohorts report some level of stress. On a scale from one to ten (where one is little to no stress, and ten is a great deal of stress), older adults report experiencing the least amount of stress at 3.3. Boomers report 4.1, followed by Gen X at 5.1, Gen Z at 5.3, and Gen Y (millennials) at 5.7. The average of all adults is 4.9.

GEN Y (MILLENNIALS) AND GEN Z SIMILARITIES

On January 17, 2019, PEW Research defined the generations for future research and discussion purposes. Officially, millennials were born between 1981 and 1996 (ages 23-38 in 2019), while Gen Z encompassed the birth years between 1997 through 2012[5] (ages 7-22 in 2019).

The Generations Defined

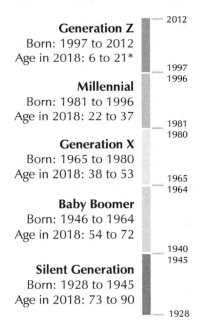

Generation Z
Born: 1997 to 2012
Age in 2018: 6 to 21*

— 2012

1997
1996

Millennial
Born: 1981 to 1996
Age in 2018: 22 to 37

1981
1980

Generation X
Born: 1965 to 1980
Age in 2018: 38 to 53

1965
1964

Baby Boomer
Born: 1946 to 1964
Age in 2018: 54 to 72

1940
1945

Silent Generation
Born: 1928 to 1945
Age in 2018: 73 to 90

— 1928

*No chronological endpoint has been set for this group. For analytical purposes, Generation Z is defined as those ages 6 to 21 in 2018.

PEW RESEARCH CENTER

FIGURE 3.2—DEFINITION OF GENERATIONS BY YEAR—DIMOCK, M. (2019). DEFINING GENERATIONS: WHERE MILLENNIALS END AND GENERATION Z BEGINS. PEW RESEARCH CENTER. JANUARY 17, 2019.

---

5   Dimock, M. (2019). Defining Generations: Where Millennials End and Generation Z Begins. Pew Research Center. January 17, 2019.

Gen Z shares common beliefs with its predecessor, the millennials. Members believe the government should do more to solve problems, that blacks are treated less fairly than whites, and increasing racial and ethnic diversity is good for the U.S. They have favorable views on interracial and same-sex marriage.

Gen Z (70%) shares the view, with millennials (64%), that the government should serve a more significant role in social and political issues. Both groups' numbers on this topic are higher than those of earlier cohorts. Gen X comes in at 53%, followed by boomers at 49% and the veterans (silent, oldest) at 39%.

On the topics of gay and lesbian marriage and interracial matrimony, Gen Z and millennials again mirror one another. Gen X, boomers, and the silent (oldest) generations trail in their opinions. The Silent generation trails at 18% and 20%, saying neither scenario is necessarily good for society.

Understanding these beliefs is important since these individuals' principles are likely to prevail for decades to come.

When we appreciate why another might feel the way they do, we can reach out to them and communicate more effectively.

OUR YOUTH GOES TO COLLEGE—SHIFTING OF LIFE PHASES; THE STUDENT DEBT DILEMMA

We have discussed the changing racial and ethnic diversity of the U.S. The minority-majority youth is the predominance of those graduating from high school.

These new graduates do not have the same financial resources as previous generations. They tend to be first-generation college students (or students from the collective underrepresented populations) who historically have not had the same financial means.

The lack of money makes it challenging to pay for college.

For those students considering an advanced diploma, the issue is usually not their parents' wealth. The question becomes: can they afford it themselves? If not, why not?

This section addresses the difficulty this new cohort experiences, given its current education debt levels. We will also consider the challenges and the implications on our society as a whole.

Correlations exist between the number of Internet webpage hits and the subsequent fall enrollments. While this information is important, it reflects a lagging indicator; it does not tell us why there may have been more or fewer webpage hits. In contrast, a leading indicator will provide information as to why something has come to be.

From this perspective, this section will examine the leading indicators to the new professional working adult learner.

Who are these students, right now? Why are they looking for a post-bachelor's degree? How do they compare to previous populations of comparable age?

Drawing from over twenty years of student data, this section focuses on who these cohort learners are and how they compare to previous groups of comparable age. The information focuses on generational cohort differences impacting—or having the potential to impact—the offering of advanced post-Bachelorette degrees.

Here are some of the issues impacting those considering advanced degrees:

- Why are college costs so high?
- What are the implications of increasing student debt loads?
- What are the implications of moving back home after graduation?
  - ▸ Postponing marriage
  - ▸ Postponing buying homes, cars, and other material possessions
- What are the implications of education and income vs. having children later in life?

Why Are College Costs So High?

As a nation, we are standing at the precipice of seismic shifts in national and international higher education and public institutions of higher education in particular. The U.S. economy is stuck in neutral since the last recession ending in 2009 (think underemployment and rising student debt). Tuition prices are skyrocketing, and student loan debt has surpassed $1.6 trillion. Parents who have leveraged their homes through equity loans and first loans, for the second time, are losing faith in the value of education as state funding is dwindling, federal grants are shrinking, and donor dollars are smaller.

These are the times in which we live. Change is inevitable. *We can continue to do what we do, until such time when we can't, and then we must do something else.* This is the prevalence of the literature today.

The average student leaving college with a B.S. or B.A. degree had $39,400 in debt in 2018, up 6% from 2017. Student debt has almost tripled and stood over $1.6 trillion in 2019. In 2018, 44% of Americans had student debt, and the delinquency rate on those loans is 11.2%. The average monthly loan repayment is $351.00. Literature suggests these obligations reduce students' opportunities for a healthy lifestyle.

In 2013, the total student debt was equal to the combined credit card and auto debt. Since then, auto debt has climbed. Now, student debt repayment is still the single largest household expense.

Colleges and universities are being forced to respond to this proliferate problem of escalating tuition. Some of these responses have been through mergers and acquisitions of educational institutions.

Those who do not address the issues will face rising costs, a declining number of new first-year students, and the financial implications of reduced revenue and increased costs.

In the end, **we cannot protect something that does not have an economic right to exist.** Market forces will prevail as they always do; free money through taxpayer's indebtedness and rising tuition does not last forever.

Moody's (in its *January Industry Outlook* reports of 2013, 2017, and 2018) was negative about the financial prospects of higher education. It highlighted the consolidation trend as one of the bolder actions by university leaders that can foster operating efficiencies and reduce overhead costs amid declining state support by centralizing such services as marketing, fundraising, purchasing, and information technology.

While colleges and universities may not see themselves as businesses, this doesn't mean they can't act like one.

In the business world, the mindset prevails: efficiencies and savings can be achieved by getting bigger and building economies of scale. This is why firms grow or merge with competitors.

But, colleges and universities are not designed to accommodate such thinking. There are fiefdoms to protect: colleges within universities, academic schools within colleges. Moreover, of course, there is tenure.

This leads to the finger-pointing about inefficiencies, which usually indicates a bloated administration and overbuilding on campus.

Some remedies to increase efficiency and reduce costs suggest:

- Limiting the number of majors and tying those remaining to the needs of the local economy.
- Offering classes year-round.
- Offering distance hybrid courses.

Other suggestions align with these standard business practices:

- Simplifying organizational structures by decreasing layers of management
- Increasing the number of direct reports for any given supervisor
- Eliminating redundancies in service organizations (IT, HR, etc.)

There is no shortage of ideas on how to fix the money problems of higher education. Over twenty-five years of the literature reveals hundreds of potential solutions.

While these are specific recommendations for colleges and universities to follow, most are nothing more than basic practices in any business/industry wanting to increase efficiencies and reduce costs. Dating back 25 years, the predominance of literature identifying and addressing inefficiencies and cost drivers include such ideas as:

- "Too many buildings..."
- "State funding has been reduced, causing increases in student tuition..."
- "Too many administrators..."
- "Spending too much on sports/football fields/arenas..."
- "Food is of too high quality and costs too much to provide..."
- "Tenure practices... [45+ years of lifetime employment]..."
- "Lack of accountability [most identified]..."
- Not a business—"...but, doesn't mean it can't be run like a business..."

Moving Back Home and Its Implications

Increasingly students (those who graduate and those who do not) are moving back home.[6] While there is no single authoritative source for actual percentages, a proliferation of studies reflects 34% of graduating students moved back home in 2011, 60% in 2013, and 56% in 2014. A follow-on survey indicated 60-85% of graduating students intended to move or had moved back home after graduation.

---

6   Fry, R. (2018). *More Adults Now Share Their Living Space, Driven in Part by Parents Living with Their Adult Children.* Pew Research Center. January 31. Retrieved from http://www.pewresearch.org/fact-tank/2018/01/31/more-adults-now-share-their-living-space-driven-in-part-by-parents-living-with-their-adult-children/

All of this seems to be due to student debt and a recovering economy with growing **underemployment** opportunities.

This trend postpones adult life phases such as getting married, having children, and purchasing material possessions typical of previous age-specific cohorts.

The manifestation of these data is that, because of student debt and economic underemployment conditions:

- 49% of graduating students have taken a job just to pay bills.
- 35% have gone back to school.
- 24% have taken an unpaid job.
- 22% have postponed having a child.
- 20% have postponed getting married.

Postponing Marriage and Children

While the question of how many college graduates return home is the subject in many studies, information on the average and median age at first marriage is readily available from U.S. government census data and reporting.

Subsequent to moving back home after graduation is the continuing (and next logical) postponement of adulthood: getting married. Again, as with moving back home, there is significant literature on the ever-increasing age at first marriage.

From 1960 to 2019, the median age for a first marriage increased nearly seven years: from 22.8 years of age to just under 30 for males, and from 20.3 to nearly 28 years for females.

College graduates are postponing marriage in record numbers. This brings up discussions on total fertility rate, education and fertility, income and fertility, and the biological implications of postponing having children.

The total fertility rate considers the number of babies the average woman would bear throughout her life if she were to survive until the end of her reproductive years and the age-specific birthrate was to remain constant.

A few quick facts on total fertility rate and its implications:

- The average American fertility rate currently sits at 1.73.
- For a country to maintain a steady population, it needs a fertility rate of 2.1.
- In 1979, the world's fertility rate was 6.0. Today, it is 2.52.

On average, the more educated a woman becomes, the fewer children she has. For example, although the U.S. average birthrate is 1.73, the rate for women with a graduate degree is 1.61.

It appears the debt load incurred with education also affects birthrate. Since 1987, when we began keeping track, the average burden on graduates has increased from $7,500 to $39,400.

There is also a direct correlation between higher income and decreasing fertility rates. The highest rate (2.04) accompanies an income under $20,000.00. When income rises to $100,000 annually, rates stabilize around 1.75%. With incomes over $100,000, there is a slight uptick to 1.83%, but far less than the highest fertility rate of 2.04.

Given young college graduates are delaying marriage, when **do** they have their firstborn? How does this compare to previous generations?

As might be expected, the median age of first-time parents has skewed upward. For mothers, this means as much as a 5% increase (to 30 years and older) while 20-30-year-old first-time motherhood decreased by 3%.

The Center for Disease Control depicts declining birthrates for three age categories: 15-19-year-olds, 20-24, and 24-29. Conversely, births for ages 30-34 years, 35-39, and 40-44 are increasing. These data align with deferring marriage and parenthood until later in life.

This shifting of the median age for children has its limits. From a biological perspective, a woman's chances of becoming infertile between the ages of 24 and 34 increase from 3% to 8%. By 35, half of all women trying to get pregnant (for over eight months) will not succeed.

By age 39, a woman has a 15% chance of being able to conceive. By a woman's 43rd birthday, her chances of getting pregnant are nearly zero.

The decrease in fertility and wanting parenthood later in life are two reasons one out of every 100 babies born in the United States is created via in vitro fertilization.

The consequences of a declining birthrate are easy to see in our rearview mirrors. Population decline comes with an increased risk of public sector bankruptcy, diminished opportunities for economic advancement, fewer opportunities for creating new businesses, and often a turn toward extreme politics.

Postponing the Purchasing of Material Possessions

As we get older, we have predictable patterns of spending, which are directly linked to life phases. When we refer to life phases, we are speaking of the scientific study of human development. The study of human development is the science seeking to understand how and why people change—and how and why they do not—as they move through different life phases.

The three domains of human development (biosocial, cognitive, and psychosocial) illustrate the developmental changes we experience as we age.

Biosocial development includes the growth and change occurring in a person's body. It encompasses the genetic, nutritional, and health factors affecting those changes, as well as motor skills: everything from grasping a rattle to driving a car.

Cognitive development includes the mental processes used to obtain knowledge or to become aware of the environment.

Psychosocial development includes temperament, emerging emotions, and social skills.

Gail Sheehy was one of the first to authoritatively document consumption patterns of individuals based on age. Harry Dent[7] aligned these patterns to accumulated data from the *U.S. Bureau of Labor Statistics Consumer Expenditure Survey.*

---

7   Dent, H. (2014). *The demographic cliff.* New York: Penguin Group.

This list summarizes Dent's findings. The consumer life cycle presented here shows U.S. Census Bureau data reflecting the median age at which Americans participate in a given event.

For example, our first homes are purchased generally around 31 years of age.

- Single (ages 18-22)
- Young Married (ages 22-30)
- First apartment (26)
- Young Family (ages 31-42)
- First home (31)
- Trade-up home (41)
- Family, kids in college (ages 46-50)
- Largest consumption of furniture (46)
- Empty Nesters (age 50+)
- College tuition peak (51)
- Purchasing autos (53)
- Retired (age 60+)
- Hospital visits (60)
- Vacation and retirement homes (65)
- Cruises (70)
- Prescription medicines (77)
- Nursing homes (84)

As we age, our family dynamic changes our demand for shelter, transportation, food, and clothing. With past generations, people generally married in their 20s, collected material possessions during the next decade, and moved toward the empty-nester phase in their late 40s.

By the time they were 50 years old, individuals had begun noticing age-related changes such as hearing loss or poor eyesight. You may have heard someone joke, "Aging is not for the faint of heart!"

Now, we are skewing traditional purchasing to later in life. 'Failure to launch' pressures the economic infrastructure designed around the historically predictable buying patterns mentioned earlier. Delaying entry into adulthood harms the whole of the U.S.

In 1950, the median age in the U.S. was 30 years of age. By 2050, it will be 40. Older citizens usually reduce their earnings. This means fewer taxes collected, which reduces the overall U.S. tax base and begins the conversation about the number of working adults (aged 16-64) needed to pay into Social Security to keep it solvent. Let us look at the historical record and a projection.

The Social Security Administration (SSA) sent its first check in 1940. At that time, there were 159.4 workers paying taxes into the system to support each retiree's disbursements. In 2010, there were 2.9 workers for each retiree's check, and the SSA predicts that, by 2034, the number of workers will fall to 2.1.

The SSA bases this prediction on two things: baby boomers retiring and the declining fertility rate failing to produce a proportionate number of new workers. This latter point is where the previous immigration discussion moves a piece into the puzzle.

Life is Challenging, Now More Than Ever

In the U.S., we have high student debt and graduates moving back home with their parents. Young people are delaying marriage, waiting to have children, and are not purchasing significant material possessions.

All of these demand action for the betterment of our society.

The root cause might be any of the previously mentioned triggers of delayed adulthood. However, this section suggests that change must err on the side of continuing to educate our populous at fair and reasonable costs.

COLLEGE ENROLLMENT IMPACT

Even our colleges and universities are scrambling to accommodate these still-to-be-fully- understood major impacts. The new demographic of the United States has had a negative impact on enrollments in higher education. Minority populations are not as prepared, financially or otherwise, to participate in higher education as the previous non-Hispanic White majority population had historically been.

From 2012-2019, enrollments in higher education were down across public and private for-profit organizations, while enrollments were slightly higher in private non-profit institutions.

These data reflect an over 1.5 million student decrease for those studying on campus.

We might ask, "Where did nearly 1.5 million students go?"

The research suggests they did not go anywhere. They do not exist. Aging and declining fertility rates are the probable culprits, once again.

Who Exactly is Going to College?—A Demographic Deeper Dive

Not every racial or ethnic cohort graduates from high school in equal numbers or enters college at the same rate. We must consider each location throughout the United States, the demographic make-up of each, and the probability of members going on to higher education.

Here is a calculation for college demand, where (l) = location; (t) = birth cohorts by year of expected high school graduation:

Demand for college (lt) =
- Probability of attendance (lt) times
- Number of children (lt)

An overlap of birthrate and social-economic factors may impact college attendance. For example, the children of high-income parents participate in at least some college at a rate of 73%, while low-income children fall to 30%.

When overlapping birth-rates with racial/ethnic factors, the data suggest:

- Asian Americans participate in some college at a rate of 84%.
- Non-Hispanic Whites participate in some college at a rate of 75%.
- Non-Hispanic Blacks participate in some college at a rate of 60%.
- Hispanics participate in some college at a rate of 60%.

Data further suggest that children whose parents have a degree are more likely (87%) to attend some college. Only 47% of those whose parents have not completed their high school education are likely to attend.

The Winds of Change—Examining the Prospects of Higher Education

There is no shortage of ideas on how to fix the declining enrollment and subsequent growing concerns of higher education. Twenty-five years of literature reveal a copious number of viable solutions.

While these are specific recommendations for colleges and universities, most are nothing more than basic practices in any business/ industry looking to increase efficiencies and reduce costs.

The greatest long-term changes are not from the low-hanging fruit. Structural changes have a lasting impact.

Rarely mentioned are the readily available structural changes to create efficiencies and reduce costs. If they are spoken about, they are seldom acted upon. These changes include such things as centralization of our decentralized colleges, elimination of programs that fail the return on investment calculation, and a second look at guaranteed lifetime employment (tenure) practices.

In looking back over twenty-five years of literature on how colleges and universities address concerns of inefficiencies and identifying and reducing cost drivers, there are dozens of topics routinely pointed out. Here are the top 10 highlights, applicable in today's world:

1. Limiting the number of majors and tying the remaining areas of study to the needs of the local economy. This topic

is discussed weekly in the literature. Government programs have been dedicated, with attendant state and federal funding, for this very purpose.

2. Reaching out to more populous parts of the country. While this was once a tactic for nearly all colleges and universities, it is now reserved for the more elite institutions. As the demographics of race and ethnicity change and the students represented in those demographics evolve, the family finances of this majority are not like prior majority cohorts. Family finances do not support moving across the country to attend a better-named college or university. Instead, newly graduated high schoolers stay closer to home.

3. More international students. This is always a windfall for the schools attracting such a group. These students historically pay the most to attend U.S. schools and receive few to no discounts.

4. Offering classes year-round. If you have ever been on a college campus in the summer, you know: you could literally throw a rock and likely not hit a soul. Numerous buildings sit mostly empty. Most colleges and universities now focus on how best to attract summer school students. With the mass production of online learning, however, students can live at home in the summer, work for pay, and refrain from attending classes on campus.

5. Online education. Where colleges and universities once fought for on-campus students, they now pursue online students. These students engage in distance learning programs, hybrid classes, online degrees, and MOOCs for credit.

6. Simplifying organizational structures. Faculty members often posit the idea of decreasing the layers of management at their school.

7. Eliminating redundancies in service organizations. This includes information technology (IT), human resources (HR), finance, or marketing through centralization and consolidation. This continues to be a major theme in organizational restructuring. Many colleges and universities have siloes, stove-piped entities creating redundant capabilities with their staffing. Moving from a decentralized organizational structure to a centralized one reduces redundant personnel and attendant costs.

8. Consolidation of colleges and universities. This is a big topic in higher education media. Currently, there is an average of 15 mergers or acquisitions per year.

9. Increased use of adjuncts, reducing the percent of tenured faculty. This is a major topic in the weekly literature and has been discussed in brief in this book. The bottom line discussion centers on three sub-topics namely: (1) tenure does not have an economic right to exist, (2) receiving guaranteed employment, guaranteed salary, an annual increase, assuming the taxpayers are willing to grant it, not having to be worried about being fired, leads to a lack of a burning platform for change and aggressively works against it, and (3) the process itself is well documented as being biased, prejudiced and inherently discriminatory.

10. Programmatic review. Eliminate small, underutilized programs that are damaging ROI. Although it seems like

common sense, reports indicate some programs dwindle to a handful of students with multiple faculty members supporting them.

The Current Supply-Demand Equation—Are We Over Educated?

You may have heard the question: "How much opportunity is there for the college-educated workforce in America's cities?"

Here are percentages for bachelor's degrees earned in the U.S. in specific years:

- 1940—5%
- 2016—31% (Another 29% had some college.)
- 2018—33%

Higher levels of education usually translate to better jobs with higher wages. However, since they require a wage premium for their knowledge and skills, candidates may find it more difficult to find a job at their skill level. Thus, the term 'underemployed' has risen over the years.

In looking at the supply and demand for higher education, the data suggest more than half of the total jobs in the United States (63%) require a high school diploma or less. This, while over 60% of the population, ages 25 and above, have more than a high school diploma. Meaning, 60% of the population of the U.S. is competing for the remaining 47% of available jobs requiring such an education.

When looking at the total share of jobs requiring college versus the percent of the total U.S. population with this level of education, we see:

- 24% of the total jobs in the U.S. require less than a high school diploma, while only 13% of the population satisfies this educational requirement.
- 39% of the total jobs in the U.S. require a high school or equivalent education, while only 27% of the population satisfies this educational requirement.
- 11% of the total jobs in the U.S. require "some college," while a full 29% of the population has this minimal level of education.
- 26% of the total jobs in the U.S. require a four-year degree or more, while 31% of the population has this minimal level of education (2016).

These data demonstrate there are more highly educated individuals than openings requiring this level of education, and there are not enough people to fill jobs needing a high school education or lower.

This implies overqualified individuals fill positions and become underemployed.

If those with college degrees take jobs requiring less education, they displace people who could have held those jobs.

Additionally, only 24% of the employers in the U.S. had a problem hiring individuals due to a lack of degree or credentials. This suggests the oversupply has led to a substantial 'up-credentialing,' which is supported when viewing data for the last 15 years.

Job 'up-credentialing' means the job has not changed, but now has a higher educational minimum credential than was previously required.

All of this implies there is a potential for diminishing returns on postsecondary education.

Underemployment—taking a job that does not require one's level of education—leads to a lower wage for the schooling attained.

CHAPTER 4

Our Aging Population—We're Getting Older Really, Really Fast

At current growth figures, the U.S. will reach roughly 400 million people in the year 2058. This is an increase from our current 329 million but shows a startling difference from 2012 projections of reaching the 400 million mark by 2040.

In five years (from 2012 to 2017), the date to reach 400 million people increased by 18 years! Although it sounds odd, the U.S. population is increasing at a decreasing rate.

This decrease is predominantly due to aging baby boomers and declining fertility rates of U.S. Caucasian females.

The baby boomers were born between 1946 and 1964. The last of the youngest boomers, those born in 1964, will turn 65 years of age in the year 2029, marking 2030 as the first year all boomers will be at least 65 years old. So, if we are lucky enough to awake on January 1, 2030, each and every one of the 78.8 million baby boomers will be at least 65 years of age. This single fact has enormous implications, sociologically, economically, and, without any doubt, demographically. This change is happening and is irreversible. People will get older.

So, when do we expect to begin to see major aging? By 2020, which is not ten years away, or even five years away, given this book is published when expected, it has already happened.

The single fastest-growing segment of the U.S. population is those individuals 55 years of age and larger... by nearly four times! We are clearly getting older, faster, as a populous.

At the same time, our average retirement age remains at roughly 62 to 63 years of age ('early' retirement, according to the SSA). This does not mean boomers don't plan to work. This generation may not want a 9:00 a.m. to 5:00 p.m. commitment, but many members look for a more relaxed and friendly work atmosphere.

RETIREMENT AND THE WORKING SENIOR POPULATION

Retirement confidence is at record lows. More than a quarter of those surveyed say they are not confident about retirement. A reported 56% of those surveyed have less than $25,000 saved in preparation for retirement, which includes savings and investments. A reported 29% have less than $1,000 saved. Although 59% of respondents said they are saving for retirement, 34% of workers and 33% of retirees tapped into their retirement savings in 2019 to cover basic expenses.

Some of the top reasons people give for delaying retirement include perceptions of a weak economy, rising health care costs, and they simply cannot afford it.

The result of this reality or perceived reality is:

- 74% of workers now plan to hold paying jobs in retirement.
- 89% report their expected retirement age has increased.
- 70% now report they expect to remain employed until at least age 65.
- 11% report predicting their retirement between the ages of 66 and 69.
- 25% report working until age 70 or above.
- 8% report they will never retire.

HIRING SENIOR RETIRED WORKERS— A WORKFORCE MULTIPLIER FOR SUCCESS

Recently, in a highly functioning organization, three people retired after 30 or more years at their company. These were productive, emotionally mature individuals with millions (and billions) of dollars of budget authority across three continents.

Throughout their careers, they experienced corporate restructuring, mergers, acquisitions, and reorganizations. One was part of the transition leadership team to merge five Fortune 100 companies with over 80,000 employees and sites in 50 states and 30 countries.

How much effort do you think it takes to manage these older workers? The answer: "Not a whole lot." It's more about leadership than management for people of this caliber. Provide the vision and remove obstacles so they can work.

This section describes the synergistic effects of hiring senior retired workers and the hidden values stemming from their significant breadth and depth of knowledge, both theoretical and experiential.

The members of this group want to stay involved as a part of the social construct while transitioning from one life phase to another. Their motivation slants toward self-actualization. There is a natural conversational flow when discussing the aging of the world's population, proposed shortfall of skilled workers in the United States, mind-set of senior retired workers, and the attendant cost implications.

There are four primary areas where this over-65 set provides advantages in a professional environment: work ethic, financial awareness, the lifetime of experience, and emotional intelligence.

Work Ethic

Retired workers have lower absenteeism and lower turnover than their younger counterparts. Some of this evolves from having fewer family obligations, such as children at home. Another reason may be that seniors use work as their social construct and have more of a commitment to it.

Productivity rises because of their exceptional dependability, better judgment, and more attention to accuracy in their work. Retirees tend to miss fewer days on the job than younger staff, and they can learn new techniques and technologies as effectively as their younger counterparts.

Financial Awareness

Perhaps because of the many economic cycles they have experienced, retired senior workers tend to be more frugal than the non-retired.

They know they will live longer than previous generations, and financial means may not carry forward to those extra years. Social Security checks play a role in their lifestyle, but seniors are aware it is under constant attack from lawmakers seeking to balance federal budgets. Financially savvy retirees keep this in mind when it comes to spending.

From an employer's perspective, hiring senior retired workers can be a financial windfall. Many in this group receive income from other sources, including SSA, pensions, and a lifetime of savings. This cohort may have medical coverage from previous employment or through Medicare. Since some seniors demand less, they cost less to employ than their younger counterparts.

Lifetime of Experience

Senior retired workers bring a lifetime of experience to new work situations. Their numerous jobs, over the years, may have spanned multiple companies or even industries.

Humans form associations—or 'memory maps'—of each setting we encounter. This helps us quickly think through the decision process when a new situation arises. The more experiences we encounter, the more memory maps we create.

It is not uncommon for retirees to find joy in sharing their learned experiences. They take great pride in calmly addressing circumstances. Where younger workers may show anxiety from not knowing how to address a problem (reacting with a level of immaturity or a heightened emotional state), senior workers can pull from their many experiences to quickly suggest alternative solutions.

Senior retired workers recognize and value their contributions. They are not destined for the CEO chair, and they seldom try to climb the corporate ladder or establish a corporate reputation. They have already 'been there.'

These men and women typically leave their egos at the door and are grateful to have an opportunity to contribute in a meaningful manner. 'CEO' is not where they wish to be, even if the opportunity presented itself.

This age-specific cohort values its ability to do what feels comfortable. In many ways, these workers realize their full potential at this point in their life and are self-actualizing. They enjoy what they do as each becomes part of a more significant social construct. They feel valued and enjoy the employment opportunities.

Emotional Intelligence

Emotional intelligence is the ability to accurately identify and understand our emotional reactions and those of others. It also involves the ability to control our emotions and to use them to make rational and informed decisions.

When discussing leadership and gender, we once relied heavily on our understanding of psychological and philosophical studies and implications. While this is still true today, there is now a growing portion of scientific study based on brain imaging.

This imaging uses tools such as positron emission tomography (PET), magnetic resonance imaging (MRI), and single-photon emission computed tomography (SPECT). These instruments allow us unparalleled insight into how male and female brains function during any number of situations. The results of these findings include neural blood flow patterns, brain structures, and brain chemistry.

Testosterone, the fight-or-flight neural chemical, is more abundant in men's bodies than in women's. Males also produce more vasopressin (territorial), while females secrete more serotonin (calming) and oxytocin (bonding).

When humans feel connected to something, the bonding comes from oxytocin. Biologists refer to this attachment as the 'tend and befriend' instinct, where higher levels of oxytocin yield lesser levels of physical aggression.

Our testosterone level links to our ability—or inability—to remain calm in a crisis, and it ties to our emotional intelligence (EI). EI is defined along four dimensions, with a total of 23 competencies.[8] Of the 23, these are the most applicable to this book:

- Self-awareness
- Self-management
- Adaptability (flexibility in handling change)

---

8   Cherniss, C., & Adler, M. (2000). *Promoting emotional intelligence in organizations*. Alexandria, VA.: American Society for Training and Development.

- Self-control (keeping disruptive emotions and impulses in check)
- Conflict management (negotiating and resolving disagreements)

Given this basic understanding of emotional intelligence, it becomes relatively straightforward to align senior retired worker characteristics to an opportunity for advanced emotional intelligence.

Beginning with a discussion on brain neural chemicals, males' (beginning at age 30) relative levels of testosterone to oxytocin change. Over time, males tend to become kinder and gentler human beings.

This supports an argument for an increasingly steady-state emotional reaction in times of crisis as well as a lessening of a need to be confrontational if challenged.

This is why we might see Dad or Grandfather becoming kinder and gentler than in previous years. Senior individuals with increasingly greater 'tend and befriend' tendencies can be fun to have around playful children.

OLDER DOES NOT MEAN DEAD

The senior population in the U.S. is living longer and experiencing healthier longevity. Although the average retirement age is just over 62 years of age, this cohort of individuals wants to remain active and productive members of society.

Today's individuals nearing retirement are reporting they don't expect to retire until at least age 66, with a full 34% saying they don't ever expect to retire. With the current and continuing shortfall in skilled labor, the senior retired workforce can play a significant role in bridging the potential gap.

Senior retired workers bring a wealth of synergistic effects to the workforce, premised on their breadth and depth of theoretical and practical experience. These individuals, through these many experiences as well as documented changes in brain neural chemicals, bring another calming effect frequently referred to as emotional intelligence. The hiring of senior retired workers can truly create a workforce multiplier for organizational growth.

PART 2: LEARNING TO LIVE AND WORK TOGETHER

CHAPTER 5

Who Will You Fight For?

FACING FEARS—YOU MOST LIKELY WILL NOT DIE, UNLESS IT IS SOMETHING THAT CAN KILL YOU

I remember being a young, skinny, and somewhat disheveled boy in fifth grade. There were tough guys. I—of course—was not one of them.

Nearly every Friday after school, a ritualistic fight occurred between the leader of the tough guys and some poor kid who, for whatever reason, didn't know enough to scurry home to avoid them.

It always happened in an empty lot, just off school property. The leader would push the chosen victim, and the brawl was on. Sometimes it didn't last too long, and other times, it would go the distance. It depended on whether the unsuspecting victim fought back. Or not.

If he did not fight back, he would receive a few slaps, maybe a punch or two to the face. It was enough to draw blood. Then he would be allowed to continue home with grass marks on his back, mussed hair, an element of blood, and forever being tagged as a cry baby (from lying on his back crying in front of the onlookers).

If there were a lot of blood, the crowd would shout for the bully to quit and let the innocent victim run home.

For those of us who were males having to pass by this location on the way home, it could be quite terrifying. The thought, as you passed by, that you could be the next victim, created fear more painful than the beating potentially received.

During this time, I was a worrywart of major proportions. I worried about everything: people not liking me, saying something to upset someone, getting sick before a test, or Friday would be my turn as the bully's victim. I worried about anything and everything imaginable.

The Friday night habit was one of my greatest worries. I did not want to be called "Pansy!" or "Cry baby!" like the others. And I certainly did not want to cry (in front of what I saw as a hundred people) while sprawled on my back being punched in the face.

The leader was the biggest kid of the bunch. Maybe he had been 'held back' several years. I didn't know, but I knew I had to walk past the empty lot each day on my way home from school. I hated Fridays and worried all week I'd be the next target.

Over the weekends, I frequently worried that next Friday I may be next. The worrying was endless. It made me sick to my stomach to think about it. In fact, it was so bad, I began to worry—around

Tuesday—that Friday was coming. I remember the feeling of total relief when a Friday came, and I managed to slip past the ensuing fight without being the next victim.

Then, one day, it happened.

I got tired of worrying.

Tired of my stomach aching for the past two years, and tired of feeling drained from fear and worry.

One day, I decided enough was enough. I could not live like this any longer. I guess I had reached my limit on worrying. It was time to free myself by facing my biggest fear.

It was time to fight the biggest and baddest bully in the group.

Here was my rationale: getting into a fight with the lead bully probably wouldn't kill me. What was the worst he could do to me? If I was the next victim, and I didn't die, what would be the outcome?

If I were the next victim and I lost—but fought a hard fight—I would be a hero for going the distance and living. If I fought a hard fight and (dare I dream?) won, I would be a hero of mega proportions.

In a fed-up-kid way, I thought, "Short of dying, I'm going to be a hero either way." I just had to overcome the fear and pain until the fight was over.

So, there it was. I was going to fight, and it was going to be this Friday after school.

My stomach ached all week. I threw up a couple of times, just thinking about it. Friday arrived. It was time. As captain of the school's safety patrols, I was one of the last people to leave. I put my captain's belt away and trudged toward the empty lot.

As I approached the already-in-progress massacre, I did the unthinkable. I pushed my way through the crowd and yelled (which came out in a squeaky voice), "Leave him alone! Get off of him you x!#@& piece of #!&&x!"

My heart pounded, and my mind was laser focused.

The crowd went silent, and I went into autopilot.

I attacked the bully.

We rolled around, swinging and punching. I got hit time and again in the face but didn't feel the punches. I swung with all I had, again and again and again. We were both swearing, and I saw blood on his face. The only thing I could think of was pounding the living sh—right out of him.

This fight wasn't just to free me from worrying.

This fight was for all who were traumatized and embarrassed and routinely pounded every Friday night for nearly two years. This fight was to the bitter end, and I wasn't going to quit until I couldn't go any farther.

There were times when he was on top of me, pounding me in the face and the side. I would kick, punch, grab, and squirm until I had a better position and then pound even harder, aiming for his face as often as I could. I don't know how long we fought, but at one point we both fell to the side, next to each other. I could barely move. We were bleeding. I looked over at him, not sure what to do next.

He spoke first. "Are we done?" I looked in his eyes and could see he was spent. So was I. "Yes," I told him. "It's over."

We got up, looked at each other with new-found respect, and started to walk away. At this moment, one of his other gang members thought he should take a stab at me, but Biggest and Baddest waved him off.

I kept thinking, "Did I really do this? Did I really confront my fears and fight the biggest bully in school?"

Spectators started cheering, patting me on the back, and saying things about my bravery and how much guts it took to do what I did. I was a hero to the on-lookers.

As the crowd dissipated, I walked away in silence. I could hear them whispering but didn't care what the other boys said. I was shaking like a leaf and beginning to feel pain. A few of the guys walked with me partway home. I wanted to cry but knew I couldn't.

I had faced my worst fear and survived. I wasn't afraid anymore. What a great feeling!

I learned a valuable lesson that day about fear. I also learned to envision the worst-case scenario and see how I would deal with it. If I could accept the worst case, the problem didn't seem so bad. And, as life progressed, I learned the worst-case scenario never materializes anyway.

As I walked home, my shirt torn, my lip and nose bleeding, I worried what my mom would say about the blood and the ripped, grass-stained clothes.

But, deep down, I had a sense of peace.

On Monday, I was the talk of the school. I was a hero! Biggest and Baddest approached me, smiled, and said, "You fight OK for a skinny guy." We became good friends, and the Friday fighting stopped (at least while I remained at the school).

A few of my teachers held me after class to talk. They were concerned I was hanging around with the wrong crowd, now, and those boys might influence me negatively. They might have been right, but I like to think I could have helped them come farther in my direction. I'll never know because we moved shortly after that.

> *My lesson, as you have probably guessed: you most likely will not die from confronting your fears. Unless, of course, they are something that can actually kill you!*

On this topic, later in life, I learned to fight without violence. I learned through my human resources experiences and my many opportunities to work with legal teams to fight through the legal system. My human resources experiences taught me how to document instances of wrongdoing. I learned the basis for discriminatory actions and how they can help protect those at a disadvantage, financially or intellectually. While there are still potholes that can stop you in your tracks, generally, having a legal basis for your fight is a whole lot better than getting punched in the face.

On this issue, if you are going to win a battle, you have to understand your opponent and what, in their opinion, they have worth losing. In identifying what they have to lose, you can more readily appeal to that particular loss as something worth entering into a compromising conversation over. In any battle I have ever fought, I learned you never get all you ask for, so to this end, you have to be prepared to compromise—to accept less.

This means we each have to understand what our positions are, versus what our real underlying interests are. Our positions are what we go in with and are asking for. Our real underlying interests, however, are the things we are really seeking; and they are usually not the same.

FIGHTING FOR SOMETHING BIGGER THAN OURSELVES

*"Courage is Being Scared to Death...
and Saddling Up Anyway"*

John Wayne once said, "Courage is being scared to death...and saddling up anyway."

Two of our four sons are attorneys.

The other two are West Point graduates who became Army Rangers. One joined the United States Army Special Forces (Green Berets), and at one point in his heroic career was the commander in charge of all Special Forces in Afghanistan. He is, without doubt, a national hero! A man above men. He and his team put their lives on the line every day, so the rest of us can work, eat, play, and sleep without worrying about evils we cannot comprehend.

(If you have a moment, please listen to the YouTube video titled Ballad of the Green Berets by Barry Sadler.)

He, like those in our police and fire departments, runs toward danger when others run away. None of them know if they will live or die, but they believe in something bigger than themselves. They believe in our nation, our way of life, and the people who make up our population: fathers, mothers, sisters, and brothers. Loved ones.

Whether we are black, white, Hispanic, Asian, young, old, gay, lesbian, citizens, or visitors: these men and women protect us from harm.

When we hear of these public servants falling in the line of duty, let us never overlook it without pause. Let us reflect on how each reacted in the face of grave danger. These are God's soldiers. The great warriors of our lives. American heroes. Feeling the fear but courageously saddling up, anyway.

There's a Coke for he and she,
And her, and me and them.
There's a different Coke for all of us—
Especially one for him.
No feet have wandered where you've walked,
No eyes saw what you've seen.
No one's lived the life you've live,
No head has held your dreams.
To act the same would be mundane—
What a boring thing to do!
That's why there is just one me
And a billion unique yous.
We all have different looks and loves,
Likes and dislikes, too—
But there's a Coke for we and us,
And there is a Coke for you.
Enjoy Yours—

—COKE ADVERTISEMENT, USA TODAY,
MONDAY, FEBRUARY 5, 2018, PAGE 1B

WE ARE MORE ALIKE THAN DIFFERENT— GENOMICALLY SPEAKING

People, places, comforts, and securities from our surroundings form our unconscious mind from birth. Since they become familiar, we have a natural desire to perpetuate them.

Interestingly, this sameness leads to the universal themes of bias, prejudice, and discrimination against those who are different. If something does not fit the mold of our secure and comfortable world, it threatens our status quo. We like sameness.

There are potential solutions that may mitigate the impact of our desire for sameness. Coupled with the recognition of proper decision-making processes and emotional intelligence, they help heighten our awareness of what we may unconsciously consider.

We are nearly identical from a biological perspective. As humans, we have one genome. For each person, it consists of approximately 21,000 genes and roughly 100 trillion cells. Most of those cells contain 23 pairs of chromosomes.

For every cell with a nucleus, there are 23 pairs of chromosomes, where the pairs contain the 3.2 billion base pairs of chemicals signified by the letters T, A, C, and G. Combinations of these base pairs form our roughly 21,000 genes. Genes (coded instructions in DNA) transmit information to our cells through RNA, telling the cells which proteins to create. Proteins keep us functioning. Understanding the makeup of each gene is the first step toward disease control.

Interestingly, we share 51% of our genes with yeast (the stuff used to make bread rise) and 98% of our genes with monkeys. Most impressively, we share 99.9% of our entire genome with other human beings. This means the only thing separating my brown hair from your blond hair, my five-foot-nine-inch stature from your six-foot-three-inch height, and my hazel eyes from your blue eyes is one-tenth of one percent (0.001) of the human genome.

One-tenth of one percent differentiates each of us from one another.

> *We are more alike than different*
> *(at least from a chemical composition perspective).*

This thought is profound and showcases this fact: there is no genomic foundation for our biases toward one another.

The thought is so profound that it reverberates and should simultaneously magnify the historical significance of our biases and prejudices, or more precisely, perhaps the insignificance our biases and prejudices should have been and why they should not have existed.

BORN WITH TWO BASIC CHARACTERISTICS

America reached an important milestone in 2011 when, for the first time, more minority babies than non-Hispanic white babies were born in a year. Going forward from 2011, most newborns have been racial minorities: Hispanics, blacks, Asians, and other non-white races. In about three decades, whites will constitute a minority of all Americans. The idea of a 'minority white' nation imparts fear among some Americans. The fear is fear of change, losing privileged status, or of having unwanted groups in their communities.

Cognitive psychological qualitative research, founded in the nurture side of the discussion, begins with a suggestion we are born with two essential characteristics: the need to survive and the need to reproduce. From these two basic instincts, psychologists (cognitive psychologists in particular) suggest we have both an unconscious and a conscious mind.

The unconscious mind—sometimes referred to as our gut feeling and survival instinct—steers us away from unsafe situations. Although our gut feeling is always 'on,' the conscious mind allows us to think through or rationalize circumstances. It may help us reach a more informed decision.

Our unconscious, intuitive, gut instinct stems from nurture-based activities. The basis for this perspective is solidly founded in several studies and is the premise for hundreds of articles and books. This animal and human ability to sense insecure conditions develops out of experiences and environmentally created scenarios.

The literature suggests, "...there are basic evolved motivations and tendencies, operating exclusively automatically up to age four when we begin developing conscious, intentional control over our minds and bodies."[9] Our deepest evolved motivations for survival and physical safety are at the root of our attitudes and beliefs.

---

9   Bargh, J. (2017). *Before You Know It*. New York, N.Y., Simon & Schuster. p. 33

Feeling safe (or avoiding threats) can be extrapolated to our sense of others. From the time of the caveman, human beings have been the most dangerous creatures around and the greatest threat to our survival.

> *"These are cues about whether people are similar to us or not. Do they look and sound the same as those around us, such as our parents, siblings and close neighbors? ...baby animals in general have an evolved general predisposition to stay close to those who are similar to them. They don't go off and play on the farmland or forest with other baby animals; instead they stay close to their own kind, the animals who are most like them who will be the ones who take care of them, give them food, provide warmth and shelter, and, most important, don't try to eat them... human beings behave more or less the same way...infants only three months old, given the choice of looking at faces of people who are the same racial-ethnic group as theirs (Caucasian) or the faces of a different racial-ethnic group (African, Middle Eastern, Asian), preferred to look at members of their own group."*[10]

BLIND SPOTS

There is a phenomenon of the human eye known as a blind spot (scotoma). This is an area, on the retina, with an obscured visual field. A particular blind spot—known as the blind point—is found where there are no light-detecting photoreceptor cells on the optic disc.

---

10   Bargh, J. (2017). p. 67.

Because there are no cells to detect light, vision is not possible. Our brain uses information from our other eye to interpolate what should go into this area. Therefore, we do not normally perceive our blind spot.

As a fun exercise with our blind spot, use this figure.

Close your right eye and look with your left eye at the plus sign in the middle.

Slowly bring the image closer to your face, continuing to look at the plus sign with your left eye.

Eventually, the left circle disappears.

What remains are the filled-in lines of the background graph.

It's as if the circle never existed.

The brain recognizes its blind spot and determines what should be in the circle's place: the checkerboard pattern. Our mind 'helps' us by removing any manifestation of our eye's blind spot.

In much the same way, our unconscious mind fills in the blanks, instinctively protecting us from harm.

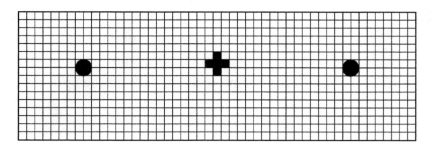

FIGURE 4.1—HUMAN EYE BLIND SPOT TEST

The blind spots in our eyes are similar to our unconscious biases.

When we have not taken the time to reflect consciously on a topic or situation, our unconscious takes over and steers us toward comfort and what we perceive to be a safer environment. Without thought, we steer away from another who doesn't look like us, or who we believe might cause us harm. Our natural instinct is to maintain sameness; sameness reduces uneasiness. Simply said, sameness makes us feel more at peace in our environment.

WHOM DO WE DISLIKE? WOW! THAT'S A LOT OF PEOPLE!

Because it is directly applicable to this section, I repeat this quote from Emo Philips:

> *Once I saw this guy on a bridge about to jump. I said, "Don't do it!" He said, "Nobody loves me." I said, "God loves you. Do you believe in God?" He said, "Yes." I said, "Are you a Christian or a Jew?" He said, "A Christian." I said, **"Me, too!"***
>
> *"Protestant or Catholic?" He said, "Protestant." I said, **"Me, too!"***
>
> *"What franchise?" He said, "Baptist." I said, **"Me, too!"***
>
> *"Northern Baptist or Southern Baptist?" He said, "Northern Baptist." I said, **"Me, too!"***
>
> *"Northern Conservative Baptist or Northern Liberal Baptist?" He said, "Northern Conservative Baptist." I said, **"Me, too!"***

*"Northern Conservative Baptist Great Lakes Region, or Northern Conservative Baptist Eastern Region?" He said, "Northern Conservative Baptist Great Lakes Region." I said, "**Me, too!**"*

"Northern Conservative Baptist Great Lakes Region Council of 1879, or Northern Conservative Baptist Great Lakes Region Council of 1912?" He said, "Northern Conservative Baptist Great Lakes Region Council of 1912."

I said, "Die, heretic!" And I pushed him over. — Emo Philips[11]

How far do we have to search to find something we do not like about another person, race, ethnicity, or other defining characteristic? What human emotions enter into this equation: anger, jealousy, envy, fear?

Here are some sobering statistics from 2017 about hate crimes. The percentages refer to the biases for which the victims were targeted:

- 59.6%: Race/ethnicity/ancestry
- 20.6%: Religion
- 15.8%: Sexual orientation
- 1.9%: A disability
- 1.6%: Gender-identity
- 0.6%: Gender bias

Our motivation for survival and physical safety is at the root of our attitudes and beliefs.

---

11   Ross, H., Tartaglione, J. & Cole, J. (2018) Our Search for Belonging: How Our Need to Connect is Tearing Us Apart. New York, N.Y., Berrett-Koehler Publishers.

Are people similar to us or not? Are they part of the in-group or the out-group?

Who should we like or trust? Who threatens our way of life?

We must ask ourselves: how do our innate beliefs influence our behaviors?

With the tectonic changes to the demographics of the U.S., what will our citizens find as a reason not to like another? Certainly, with the changes to age, race, and ethnicity, there will be sufficient reason to dislike, if society looks to do so.

Scientific, historical accounts reflect *Homo sapiens*, essentially our human evolutionary ancestry, has only existed for a meager 300,000 years in the 4.6 billion years since the origin of the Earth. During this short stint in history, we have experienced an unending series of conflicts.

Recorded history is replete with these many human conflicts—conflicts premised on differences in religion, ethnicity, race, gender, geography, and so many more. Our very limited circumference of trust is illustrated even here in our great United States, through a myopic lens and ethnocentric minds-eye. Whom should we like? Whom should we trust? Whom should we not like and/or trust?

In the end, who is the next person or group individually or collectively threatening our survival?

Fast forward post-college and through nearly thirty successful years in the defense industry. I decided to go to work for my alma mater. I was very fortunate to have been given the opportunity to build a for-profit entity within our non-profit public university. While building the organization had all the normal long days and nights, as well as the gratification of success, it was something entirely different I found hilarious and sad at the same time.

When I moved from business/industry to higher education, I was told by friends on both sides to be prepared for an environment like I've never seen before. After a few short months, then years, I noticed what appeared to be an unending somewhat confrontational attitude from others, not all, but some.

As one friend told me, others' feelings were your papers weren't published in as prestigious journals as mine were, your books don't have the circulation mine have, your conferences aren't as large as the ones I attend, and, oh yes, your mother doesn't dress you as well as my mother dresses me.

Really?! Are you serious?! How far do we have to look to find something we don't like about another person? I mean, who cares? Does it really matter if my mother doesn't dress me as well as yours dresses you?

BIAS AS AN UNCONSCIOUS BEHAVIOR

Bias can be an unconscious behavior we do not realize we are employing. There are hundreds of studies backing this claim. Three, in particular, replicated numerous times, demonstrate this point:

- Buying wine—People in supermarkets buy more French wine when French music is playing and more German wine when German music plays.
- Tenure screens—More interviews were offered to those with male names than with female names, regardless of qualifications (even when qualifications were switched).
- Lab techs—Scientists set the pay level lower if a job seeker had a female name. The supervisors had not seen the candidates.

Our unconscious mind synchronizes and coordinates the billions of pieces of information per second.

"All of us are bombarded by information, an estimated 11 billion bits of it per second. But we can process just 40 bits per second. So our brains take shortcuts...for our early ancestors, this was literally a lifesaver.

If a caveman walked out of his cave and saw an animal, he couldn't take the time to consciously process that it had fur, so it wasn't a human; and strong legs, so it must run fast; and sharp teeth, so it must be a carnivore; and...oh, wait, it must be a tiger. By the time he consciously assessed all that, he'd be lunch."[12]

In reexamining our unconscious mind, how might we stop compensating for our blind spots?

The best guideline: stop and think before acting.

Are we behaving in a way that passes the test of logic and rational thought? Or, are we simply acting out of instinct?

---

12   Lipman, J. (2018). That's What She Said. New York, N.Y., Harper Collins Publishers.

THE QUANTITATIVE SIDE OF THE DECISION-MAKING PROCESS

We can discuss decision making as both quantitative and qualitative processes. The literature on both is overwhelming. When I search Amazon for books with the titles or keywords *decision making*, it returns nearly one-quarter of a billion hits. That's a lot of literature for any subject!

The intent in this section is to heighten awareness of subconscious and unconscious qualitative behavioral characteristics at the root of groupthink, bias, and inherent discrimination. This segment does not discuss tools and techniques for making good decisions, but instead, how to lay a foundation for understanding the approaches to making better, more informed decisions.

Management science is the quantitative discipline for making better decisions. This approach capitalizes on the extensive use of quantitative analysis. Management science is also known as operations research. Many use the terms management science and operations research interchangeably.

Problem-solving is the process of identifying a difference between the actual and the desired state of affairs, then taking action to resolve the difference. For problems significant enough to justify the time and effort of careful analysis, the process involves these seven steps:

- Identify and define the problem.
- Define the set of alternative solutions.
- Define the criterion or criteria used to evaluate the alternatives.
- Evaluate the alternatives.
- Choose an alternative.

- Implement the selected alternative.
- Evaluate the results. Was a satisfactory solution reached?

Decision making is the term generally associated with the first five steps of the problem-solving process. Thus, the first step of decision making is to identify and define the problem. Decision making ends with the choosing of an alternative solution, which is the act of making the decision.

Quantitative analysis provides a framework to evaluate selected alternatives based on sound, rational, and methodical thought processes. The management science approach is taught in colleges and universities worldwide and usually involves one or more semesters of study.

THE QUALITATIVE SIDE OF THE DECISION-MAKING PROCESS

On the qualitative side of the decision-making discussion, there is probably nothing more read in recent times than the work on emotional intelligence (EI). EI has been researched and reported on as the foundation for reliable, thoughtful decisions.

There are four dimensions of emotional intelligence. Within the dimensions of emotional intelligence (self-awareness, self-management, social awareness, and relationships management), there are eighteen competencies. They are the vehicles of primal leadership. Even the most effective leader will not have them all but will exhibit at least one competency from each of the domains.

The literature on decision making is significant. The number of books on quantitative to qualitative foundational skills is voluminous. The discussion on decision making naturally progresses to leadership traits and characteristics, and leadership is mentioned when talking about decision making. The very essence of leadership and management is premised on qualitative characteristics.

> *Before we can consciously make good decisions, we must train ourselves to recognize when we are about to make an unconscious decision that might require further thought.*

BUSINESS CASE FOR DIVERSITY AND INCLUSIVITY: IT'S ALL ABOUT GROWTH

Several years ago, we were required to attend 'diversity training' (now termed 'diversity and inclusivity'). In almost every case, this was one of the most boring discussions we could have. It centered on the legal aspects of not being sued for discrimination in the workplace. The human resources team or legal department usually gave the presentation nobody wanted to attend. There was nothing positive about the training, and—year after year—it never changed.

Nevertheless, it was necessary. Company performance and profitability were tied to legal repercussions from lawsuits. Most of us knew there had to be a better way to express the value of diversity in the workforce other than just 'avoiding litigation.' We desperately wanted a concept or model that could resonate with each employee.

Then, around the late 1990s, the concept of diversity in the workforce took a decidedly different turn. We began talking about diversity as more than merely a race or gender issue and started looking at it as an array of diverse characteristics representing the general employee population.

The familiar things associated with age, race, gender, religion, physical ability/disability, and national ethnicity were still identified (as they should be).

However, additional characteristics all came into the fold: family situation, sexual orientation, veteran status, language spoken, work experience, education, geographical location, functional discipline, and international experience. Each contributed toward a more encompassing perspective of diversity.

The identification of these additional characteristics also ushered in a new perspective. Now we talked about:

- Diversity being imperative for business survival.
- Diverse teams making better decisions, which made us more competitive.
- Creating an atmosphere to help great ideas thrive.
- Celebrating our uniqueness.

During this time, we also talked about creating an inclusive culture and creating metrics for measuring the business results. Most organizations talked about strategic objectives and hiring and promoting at all levels.

These objectives included recognizing, developing, and using diverse employee talent, increasing the use of mentoring, building relationships and alliances with local communities and highly diverse colleges and universities, and creating a bidirectional line of open and honest communication.

Numerous programs and initiatives supported our strategic objectives. Things were starting to solidify in terms of actions and commitments, and we realized we were now years beyond our previous training. We had moved away from compliance-related exercises and into logical reasoning to increase growth in our organizations.

Around 1999, I attended an NAACP luncheon in our city. It provided additional insight into the value of diversity, and the workshop stirred my emotions. Halfway through the session, I phoned my boss, saying I wanted to start a diversity council at work. Thankfully, he was always open to new initiatives. He told me, "Go ahead and do it. Sounds great to me."

And I did.

I pulled the demographics from our facility and selected the individuals to represent the employees on our first council. Mindful of staying with our philosophy of diversity being about more than just compliance, I selected representatives from as many of the different characteristics as I could find.

I wasn't sure what to expect.

One of the first questions asked in the opening session was, "Isn't diversity supposed to be about gender and race?" If our own team couldn't differentiate between diversity as the company defined it, the general population was certainly going to be confused!

We looked at one another in silence, sort of afraid to say anything. We didn't want to hurt each other's feelings, and we certainly didn't want to say something that sounded biased or prejudicial. And none of us wanted to show how little we knew of the concept.

After a brief period of awkwardness, someone asked how we should refer to different races and ethnicities. Was it 'Black' or 'African-American?' Was it 'Mexican' or 'Hispanic?'

Most of us weren't sure, but we wanted to know.

So, for our first homework assignment (if you will), we searched why we would use one reference over another. We discovered some terms originated with the government or were part of political or religious movements, while others were historical and passed down from one generation to the next. We also found there was a difference between race and ethnicity.

In the end, we all felt a little more comfortable with this complex unknown new world. We worked together to learn the terms that differentiated us.

Having grown up in a diverse neighborhood, I never felt animosity toward an entire diverse characteristic. However, I'm not saying I didn't like certain people if they were mean or threatening.

Fast forward to today. Those we call Gen X, millennials, and Gen Z really do 'get it.' They are the most accepting of differences in people. In fact, most in these three groups don't see any value in even discussing varying diversity characteristics representative of prior older initiatives and programs. They already accept the differences.

As I travel the country giving awareness presentations, I routinely hear stories that are indicative of how open these cohorts are to diversity. At no time has anyone in any of these three cohorts led me to believe they doubted the significant contributions of prior models of training, awareness heightening, and education attendant to diversity and inclusion. They take it for granted: all people are their friends, colleagues, parents, or grandparents. Inclusivity and acceptance is their norm, as I hope someday will be the case for all human beings.

CHAPTER 6

Legal Implications on Changing Demographics—Can We Legislate it?

'Legislation' implies we have solidified our understanding of an issue sufficiently to define the terms and the laws. In a chicken-and-egg discussion, our initial inaction can promote legislation. Legislation can also promote change, especially as it relates to our corporations and communities. This chapter lays the foundation for the next two chapters.

BIAS AND INHERENT DISCRIMINATION, COERCION, GROUPTHINK

Bias and inherent discrimination are modeled in this story from a conference at a high research university. A one-day symposium on hiring females and underrepresented minorities focused on the unconscious bias of faculty search-and-screen committees. Associate deans, department heads, dean leadership teams, and the deans themselves participated.

The presenter expressed concern about our nationwide issue of search-and-screen committees' built-in prejudice. She explained this is seen in ratios of females and underrepresented minorities on the tenure track or as (current) tenured faculty. The speaker presented several studies on this issue, noting that one demonstrated how names alone influenced a committee on whether a candidate was qualified. Where credentials were comparable, candidates with black-sounding names were rated lower than those with white-sounding names.

Seeing the bigger picture is similar to the concept of open versus closed systems. In a closed system, the organization or unit only sees within itself, whereas in an open system, the organization takes into consideration the external environment.

In the open system, the company considers the multitude of outside factors influencing it, from environmental to competition with other similar firms within a given industry.

In examining tenure practices, the lecturer noted: individuals who make up the system are those who decide the fate of potential tenured faculty. This self-contained structure is, by definition, a closed system, and newly tenured faculty may be indistinguishable from the current group.

Coercion is the practice of forcing someone to act involuntarily by using threats, intimidation, or some other form of pressure or force.

It includes forceful actions—to induce the desired response—that violate the free will of an individual. Coercion is a crime of duress.

Groupthink is a psychological phenomenon where the desire for harmony or conformity results in an incorrect or deviant decision-making outcome. Members minimize conflict by reaching a consensus without critical evaluation of other ideas or viewpoints. They isolate themselves from outside influences. Loyalty keeps individuals from raising controversial issues or alternative solutions.

With coercion or groupthink, the closed system promotes a single-minded outcome. This can result in bias and prejudice against those who do not meet the identity of the voting group. Most likely, it ends in a "No" vote based on a subjective qualification.

WHAT DOES PREJUDICE LOOK LIKE?

Prejudice is an irrational and inflexible opinion formed from limited and insufficient knowledge. Stereotypes often give rise to prejudice, with exposure to distorted and rigid images of a particular set leading us to prejudge anyone we identify with the group.

The unconscious mind of the individuals in a closed system may extend beliefs, biases, and prejudices against those who are not like them. This can contribute to the lack of representation, from different genders and minorities, in a company.

Similar minds think alike. Similar minds in a closed system, through micro-inequities and preconceived biases (and perhaps through coercion and groupthink), provide the opportunity for discrimination.

WHY DON'T YOU LIKE ME?

An Example from Higher Education— Sameness Perpetuates Sameness

A friend of mine is from a prestigious public university. It is ranked in the top 100 worldwide. In a recent conversation with her, she was visibly upset.

One of the colleges at her university had hired 12 new tenure-track faculty members. There were no females or minorities among them. "Not one! Not even one!" she exclaimed.

She asked her college's dean, "How is it that not one female or minority wanted to come to work for one of the highest-rated, most prestigious universities in the world? How could this be?"

He replied, "The academic department heads are responsible for the faculty hires, and they failed to hire females or minorities."

She didn't know who she blamed the most: the University for allowing this to happen, the dean, or the academic department heads that stood by and said they were not in charge of the search and screen committee (it was the faculty's responsibility).

She was deeply bothered by this feeling of sameness perpetuating sameness.

Prejudice in Action—Purdue Wins 72-63, Not That it Matters

Prejudice is a preconceived perception with no actual experience or factual information. It is a function of ignorance. Period! I now understand this.

Stereotypes often give rise to prejudice. We tend to assign to every individual in a given population the same perception, again, simply based on preconceived notions without any factual or first-hand knowledge.

At one point in my career, I played into the ignorance.

I was the head of the Human Resources department of a company with roughly 7,000 employees across multiple states. During this time, I received a phone call from someone at Indiana University (IU).

He left a message asking me to become a member of his Executive MBA Industry Advisory Board. I thought there was no way in the world I would ever be a part of anything at IU. I was a graduate of Purdue University (PU), and we were fierce competitors.

I didn't respond.

During my collegial days at Purdue, IU and PU were bitter enemies. This stemmed from our highly competitive basketball programs. Bobby Knight was the head basketball coach at IU when Gene Keady served in that role at Purdue.

These two guys were fierce competitors. In one instance, as I understand it, Bobby Knight brought a mule onto his weekly show and made the statement Gene was invited but was not able to come, so he sent his second in command or some similar degrading remark. I heard Coach Knight also made statements and jokes like, "How do you know when it is prom night at Purdue? You can tell by how many tractors are lined up at Dairy Queen..." Ugh!

To say our two schools were fierce competitors is similar to saying the Grand Canyon is simply a pothole in the street. Students from both schools seriously disliked (which I'll say since I recognize 'hate' is such a strong word) each other. IU's basketball team had won six national championships. Purdue's only national basketball championship was in 1932!

You may remember the historic game on February 23, 1985, and Bobby Knight's chair-throwing incident. IU was expected to win, but Coach Keady had a different idea. As with most meetups between the teams, it was a close, back-and-forth nail biter.

At one point, Coach Knight got extremely angry, stomped back and forth. What he did next has gone down in collegiate basketball history (and become the butt of many jokes).

He grabbed a bench chair and heaved it across the IU frontcourt.

It bounced and twirled around, skidded past the free-throw line, and slid next to people on the opposite sideline. Stunned fans all over the arena started screaming, and the uproar was deafening. I was watching the game on TV and began yelling, "He should be tossed from the game! He could have hit one of our players with that chair!" The referees agreed.

Even his leaving the game took several minutes as Coach Knight dawdled and moseyed across the floor to the exit. He brushed shoulders with the ref who threw him out, which in itself was a major violation. No one is allowed to intentionally bump into a referee, especially out of anger.

Games like this—and there were many—created the intense rivalry between our two schools.

So, after three attempts to reach me, the guy from IU made the statement, "Look, I know you graduated from Purdue. But, if you would only call me back and give me a chance, I think you will see not all people from IU have red eyes and green horns." Reluctantly, I did call him back. He invited me to visit the IU campus, and, in the end, I did join his Executive MBA Board and visited IU many more times after that. IU is a beautiful campus. There is a restaurant that serves the greatest meatballs and steaks, which I always try to visit when there.

When our two head coaches retired, so did my intense ill feelings for IU. I really didn't dislike IU or its graduates. I disliked Coach Knight's antics.

Now, after having visited there several times and gaining new friends, I liked going to the campus in Bloomington, Indiana, more than I ever thought I would.

Those years are eons ago, it seems. I can't imagine not feeling normal feelings for IU or the many people I know who graduated from there.

By the way, Purdue won that infamous game 72 to 63! Not that it matters.

And oh! I heard Coach Knight opened a furniture store, and if you bought a couch, he'd throw in a chair!

Sorry. I couldn't help myself.

FIGURE 6.1—MEN'S 1932 NATIONAL CHAMPIONSHIP
BANNER DISPLAYED IN MACKEY ARENA

OUR LEGISLATIVE ENVIRONMENT PROMOTES CHANGE

More than anything else, the legislative environment has prompted interest and change in our diversity actions and practices in our social, corporate, and personal lives.

If we consider the legislative environment of managing diversity, we see these seminal events:

- The Equal Pay Act of 1963 (EPA), protecting men and women (who perform substantially equal work in the same establishment) from sex-based wage discrimination
- The Civil Rights Act of 1964 (Title VII), which prohibits employment discrimination based on race, color, religion, sex, or national origin
- The Age Discrimination in Employment Act of 1967 (ADEA), which defends individuals who are 40 years of age or older
- Sections 501 and 505 of the Rehabilitation Act of 1973, which ban discrimination against qualified individuals with disabilities who work in the federal government
- Title I and Title V of the Americans with Disabilities Act of 1990, as amended (ADA), which prohibit employment discrimination against qualified individuals with disabilities in the private sector and state and local governments
- The Civil Rights Act of 1991, which, among other things, provides monetary damages in cases of intentional employment discrimination
- Title II of the Genetic Information Nondiscrimination Act of 2008 (GINA), which disallows employment discrimination based on genetic information about an applicant, employee, or former employee

Each of these legislative acts spawned numerous initiatives, actions, and movements, as discussed in the following chapters.

CHAPTER 7

Corporate and Community Efforts— Can We Organize It?

The topic of corporate and community efforts dates back long before today's definition or the materialization of diversity councils, committees, legislation, or any real definition—or understanding—of our numerous differences.

As children, most of us learned a song that went something like this:

In fourteen hundred and ninety-two, Columbus sailed the ocean blue.

It was a courageous thing to do, but someone was already here.

Columbus knew the world was round, so he looked for the East while westward bound. But he didn't find what he thought he found, and someone was already here.

The Inuit and Cherokee, the Aztec and Menominee, the Onondaga and the Cree; Columbus sailed across the sea, but someone was already here.

The point being, someone was already here when Columbus arrived in the West Indies. This was also the case when Amerigo Vespucci—an Italian explorer, financier, and merchant—first made notice of what became our present-day America.

As you may recall from earlier discussions, historical accounts reflect *Homo sapiens*, our human evolutionary ancestry, has only existed for a meager 300,000 years, originating in the, now, continent of Africa. So, everyone who moved out of Africa and into Europe, Asia, and the Americas, was at one point, different. Maybe the first to arrive somewhere weren't different, but everyone after that was. At least they were perceived as intruders, newcomers, or simply different.

The United States of America continues to be the most diverse nation in the world. Early settlers came from France, Spain, the Netherlands, and England. By the mid-1800s, Germany, Ireland, and Northern and Western Europe were added to the list. Before 1900, immigrants arrived from Russia, Italy, and Eastern and Southern Europe.

Today, most immigrants are from China, India, and Mexico, with considerably more from Asian than Hispanic descent predicted for the coming decades.

From the beginning, we have been one of the most diverse nations in the world. Today, our mosaic is composed of people from all nationalities, races, and ethnicities. Our collective diverse strength makes our nation prosperous.

CORPORATE SHIFTS IN UNDERSTANDING AND BEHAVIORS

Each of the legislative events mentioned earlier spurred a change in our thinking about diversity and our corporate practices, initiatives, and policies influencing our diverse behavior. There are four overlapping periods in our attitudes and behaviors as they relate to diversity and inclusivity.

First: During the 1960s and 1970s, we focused on legislation and compliance. Our corporations offered training and education centered on the legal and financial aspects of being sued. Corporate focus frequently erred on the side of avoiding negative optics and their subsequent costly, sometimes publicly embarrassing lawsuits. There was no connection made between this approach to training our workforces and the underlying business case for practicing an inclusive culture.

Second: Our corporate focus shifted in the early 1980s to the concept of assimilation. During this period, corporate training helped us understand how best to bring women and minorities into our workplaces. We looked at hiring, search-and-screen, and onboarding practices. During the latter portion of the 1980s, corporations began using the term 'diversity' in our training and development activities.

Third: From the late 1980s through the 1990s, corporate focus again shifted. This time, it moved toward recognizing our many differences, having sensitivity training, and taking a first look at the business case for diversity and inclusion.

Fourth: Most of today's literature emphasizes business success, profitability, and growth. This approach brings with it the new term 'inclusion.' Inclusion recognizes our differences and seeks to capitalize on them.

Earlier, I mentioned the concept of diversity in the workforce taking a decidedly different turn around the late 1990s.

We began talking about diversity as more than merely a race or gender issue and looked at it as an array of diverse characteristics representative of our general employee population.

We identified the familiar things associated with age, race, gender, religion, physical ability/disability, and national ethnicity.

However, additional qualities such as family situation, sexual orientation, veteran status, language spoken, work experience, education, thought, geographical location, functional discipline, and international experience contributed toward a more complete perspective of variety in the workplace.

Identifying these additional characteristics ushered in training material with a different slant. Now we talked about:

- Diversity being crucial for business survival.
- Diverse teams making better decisions, which made us more competitive.

- Creating an atmosphere to help great ideas thrive.
- Celebrating our uniqueness.

During this time, we moved away from compliance-related training into logical reasoning attendant to increasing growth in our organizations.

COMMUNITY ENGAGEMENT AND MOVEMENTS

Today, we have a highly sensitized population. The advent of social media has provided instant visibility into social vignettes, with equal instantaneous opportunities for creating collections of people with similar interests and concerns.

A quick Google search provides over 116 social movements. While not all happened before the mass utilization of social media, many have. Examples include the rapid climb and dissemination of information around movements such as Black Lives Matter, LGBTQ, Me Too, and the Pro-Life and Pro-Choice undertakings.

As part of the world community, Americans now have the opportunity to heighten awareness and address social connections where we wish to bring people together.

In nearly every major community across our country, cities and towns have joined together to recognize their differences. The residents of these districts establish acceptable norms, practices, and values statements.

One such example comes from three adjoining government entities near my alma mater: Lafayette, West Lafayette, and Tippecanoe County in Indiana. These three entities came together in 2000 to establish The Diversity Roundtable. The roundtable is their position on diversity, the way they support it, and how they demonstrate their appreciation for the value of being different.

The mission of The Diversity Roundtable is to

- "Work toward inclusion by encouraging equity, access, and respect for all."
- "Commit to multiple dimensions of human diversity, specifically those linked to conditions in our community that result from prejudice and discrimination."
- "Provide leadership and promote strategies to achieve a culture that values diversity as evidenced by attitudes, policies, and practices within Lafayette, West Lafayette, and Tippecanoe Country, Indiana."

The roundtable holds monthly meetings and supports and promotes diversity summits, groups, and political action committees attendant to diversity. This is but one example of major multi-city involvement in recognizing, assimilating, and applying principles related to diverse populations.

CHAPTER 8

Our Personal Responses—Can We Embrace It?

"I WANT TO BE A LAWYER."

As a child, I came to resent the constant stream of bill collectors. They would call endlessly, day and night, sometimes several times within a few minutes. They repossessed our car on Christmas Eve, forcing my grandpa to come to get us so we could go to Grandma's for our annual celebration (which I loved). As I perceived them, those collectors were sneaky, low-life human beings.

During this challenging time, my mom worked for a bank and sought guidance from one of its attorneys. I went with her to visit him one day. I was awestruck by the grandeur, the pomp and circumstance, if you will, of the tallest building in our city.

The bank occupied the main floor and was immediately visible when you entered the building. It was a grand entrance with painted murals on the ceilings, pillars, and other testaments to strength and integrity.

There was a soda shop inside the building to the right of the main entrance. It sold coffee, newspapers, and a few snacks.

As we entered the attorney's office, I looked out the windows. People looked like ants crawling along on the sidewalks several floors below. Across the street was the full-of-grandeur courthouse. It was big, with massive pillars. It was the embodiment of what law represented.

I decided I wanted to help people, too, like her attorney was helping us. These people were dragon slayers fighting a world we knew nothing about. Theirs was, in my opinion, the noblest of all professions. My mom said she would talk with her lawyer and ask if I could shadow him in a court hearing. He agreed.

When the day came, Mom and I sat in the back of a courtroom to watch the proceedings. It was amazing! It was formal, where only the best and brightest could participate. I wanted to be part of the language, formality, and the judge presiding with ultimate authority.

I told Mom, "When I grow up, I want to be an attorney." In my heart, I believed this was the best way for me to protect those less capable—to fight against the injustices of the world. I wanted to play their game on their court and win the battles of legal war. In my young mind, I was destined to be a lawyer!

Perhaps this explains why I encouraged two of our sons to become attorneys. I have a life plan that takes me to the grand old age of 103.

While life doesn't always go as planned, sometime between now and then, I plan to go to law school as well. We'll see.

CHANGE MANAGEMENT—PEOPLE, THE HARDEST PART

Change is an inevitable part of the human experience, and it occurs every day. What causes us, as humans, to react differently than usual is when change happens at a pace different than the average pace of change. In other words, the speed of change, in some instances, is the first recognition of the difference that heightens our awareness of it. Our subsequent behavior is a manifestation of this realized change.

Whether we are talking about adjustments in business and industry, higher education, or society at large, the concepts of the change process and our human reactions to it are generally the same.

Since change happens all the time, this chapter discusses its management. It is similar to starting a new program with a new team, but our topic is the demographics of our nation.

We must discuss change management as it impacts individuals involved in a new endeavor or experience. A demographic transformation invokes—as with all change—an emotional response.

While it is essential to understand the vision, goals, and objectives of variation (as well as the processes to move it into the business environment), managing the emotional impact is vital. A Google search for 'culture trumps strategy' reveals numerous organizations, CEOs, and book authors using the phrase. Maintaining a healthy perspective while initiating and managing the currents of change is critical.

ACTIVITIES OR PHASES OF THE CHANGE MANAGEMENT PROCESS

Change is not the same thing as transitioning. Change is situational—for example, a new boss, a new office, or even a new process.

Transition, on the other hand, is a process with activities and the associated products or outcomes from those activities. Transitions can be extremely emotional and have the potential for upheaval. Individuals in transition are likely to experience emotions similar to those found while grieving.

There are challenges to leaving former business processes behind. Depending on the situation, these trials may include shifting emotional ties, accepting new infrastructure, and working with the organizational changes involved with new people, processes, practices, and methodologies.

Things as simple as filling out a travel expense report can become an emotionally charged process change.

During this initial phase, we should recognize the potentially crippling personal effect of the process (likened to Kübler-Ross model of grieving):[13]

- Denial   "This cannot be happening."
- Anger   "Why do we have to go through this?"
- Bargaining   "What if we simply did…?"

---

13   Bridges, W. (2009). *Managing transitions: Making the most of change.* Philadelphia, PA: Perseus Books Group.

- Depression   "Things will never be the same. I want it to stay the same."
- Acceptance   "I recognize my limited ability to change it. So, let's make do."

It is important to recognize that individuals in different circumstances see their losses differently during this phase.

Some may have a better education; others may envision more opportunities, and those closing in on retirement may feel less impact than their coworkers.

During this time, exaggerations may become commonplace. Overreacting is not the same for everyone. Keep in mind: people react to what they perceive as a loss. Usually, the losses—not the changes—cause issues. Each person sees a piece of their world going away, but it may not be the same piece others are losing.

Anyone, when dealing with a stressful situation impacting their ability to provide for themselves or their family, could exaggerate and overreact. It may help to remember what we call 'overreaction' is just a normal response to stress. It is something we can anticipate.

What this book is attempting to do is to help heighten awareness of why the transition is taking place. What is it that seems to cause us pause, varying feelings of uncertainty, feel that things are different? "What is going on here?" as the saying goes.

Assuming we gain some level of understanding, we can ideally come to see how the change may impact us individually. In this instance, how the changing face of our nation becomes something very personal to us. Seeing this bigger picture may help us be more accepting.

> *Our world is not crumbling; it is simply continuing to change, perhaps in a manner that elicits our unconscious uneasiness.*

MANAGING OUR PERSONAL CHANGE

We no longer live with long periods of stability, followed by short bursts of change. We are in a period of constant evolution, as a nation and in our personal lives.

Just by watching recent news on TV, we may feel anxiety, exhaustion, fear, frustration, or depression. If this is the case, we may also experience lower productivity.

Self-efficacy is the belief we can succeed in a given situation or accomplish a given task. We base our level of self-efficacy on the belief we have the necessary resources (mental, physical, and financial) to accomplish the work placed before us. As we prosper, we gain confidence. This sureness then feeds our conviction that we will succeed in similar situations.

The stronger our perceived self-efficacy, the higher the goals we set for ourselves and the firmer our commitment to them. People with low self-efficacy are easily convinced their effort in the face of difficulties is futile. They quickly give up trying. Those with high self-efficacy view impediments as challenges to overcome.

This book helps us understand these changes and gain some personal control over our feelings and thoughts.

FEAR CAN EQUALLY STIFLE ACTION

I am Fear. I am the menace that lurks in the paths of life, never visible to the eye but sharply felt in the heart. I am the father of despair, the brother of procrastination, the enemy of progress, the tool of tyranny. Born of ignorance and nursed on misguided thought, I have darkened more hopes, stifled more ambitions, shattered more ideals and prevented more accomplishments than history could record.

Like the changing chameleon, I assume many disguises. I masquerade as caution. I am sometimes known as doubt or worry. But whatever I'm called, I am still fear, the obstacle of achievement.

I know no master but one; its name is Understanding. I have no power but what the human mind gives me, and I vanish completely when the light of Understanding reveals the facts as they really are, for I am really nothing."

You see, if you have the courage to acknowledge your fears, you will be taking the first step toward controlling them instead of them controlling you. And if you take the next step toward understanding, you will be able to move past them to empathy, perhaps even to love. —Lou Tice *(The Pacific Institute. November 17, 2016)*

Fear is a natural emotional state, causing people to act or, in some cases, to not act. It can create scenarios where important decisions are not made. Fear and its implications are well documented.

Fear does not go away. It is always with us. It exists in every new attempt or lack of attempt. Fear exists in every job change, move, promotion, or challenge. Fear can keep us from succeeding to higher levels in our lives and careers.

Just as was the case when confronting the bully at school, one way to deal with fear is to visualize the worst-case scenario. Ask, "How would I deal with X should it materialize?" If you can visualize facing, experiencing, and resolving the situation, you gain a sense of control and power over the fear.

My questions were, "What can happen? If we fight, is it going to kill me?" I correctly surmised the answer was, "No," so I had to find a new worst-case scenario!

The worst-case rarely materializes. The actual occurrence usually has a lesser impact than we feared. Once we feel a sense of power over a situation, we can confront it and more readily address the fear associated with it.

I once knew a guy who was an electrical engineer with two advanced degrees. But his competence didn't stop his fear. Was he going to lose his job to a company lay off? This fear froze his ability to make purchasing decisions.

He came to me with his concerns, and I shared, "Think outside the city limits, to the county, the state, and our region of the country. If you think about the entire U.S. instead of this one office, you'll see an unending demand for your talent and credentials." His opportunities were limited only by his personal decisions. Once he saw this bigger picture, he said he felt better and more at ease. He realized his fears were manifests of his limited vision. He was at peace.

What do we fear? Is it truly justified? Can we see the bigger picture? Can we take control of it?

Conclusion

How deep do we have to look to find something we do not like about another person, race, ethnicity, or other defining characteristic? What human emotions enter into this equation: anger, jealousy, envy, fear?

As I look back through the years and the evolution of my personal life, perhaps I wasn't liked as a younger individual because of where I grew up. Maybe it was my association with others of varying races and ethnicities. Or how I dressed (you might recall I grew up in relatively poor circumstances). Perhaps you feared me because of my social-economic class. Or you didn't trust me for similar reasons.

As I moved to a better part of town (but still lived in a lower home setting), perhaps you didn't like me for a whole other set of reasons, or even the same set of reasons, yet simply in a different environment. Perhaps when I joined higher education, even after a tremendously successful thirty-year career in the highly competitive defense industry, you still didn't like me because you wished you had my kind of career.

Maybe it was because you felt my scholarship was less than yours, or—as I joked earlier—my mother didn't dress me as well as your mother dressed you.

I'm not sure. I am not a psychologist or a psychiatrist. I'm just a person, like you, trying to make a living, enjoy this one life I've been given, share times with friends and family, and get ahead in my career to be able to better afford some of the things we all need and want.

I am *just* a person, imperfect, yet someone who shares 99.9% of our collective DNA with all other *Homo sapiens*; people, just like you and me.

"Why Don't You Like Me?" was written to heighten awareness of the many changes happening in and around us. These changes impact our society, our businesses, our educational institutions, our homes, our heads, and our hearts.

"Why Don't You Like Me?" was written to help us to see another's perspective. To understand these seemingly unrelated 'things' are—in fact—related.

These many circumstances, whether it's the changing racial and ethnic face of our nation, the delaying of marriage, home buying, and having children of our youth, the capitalization of our retiring workforce, or, the cultural difficulty of accepting, are happening now, at this time, and are not going to resort back to a previous time.

CONCLUSION

These many changes are real.

Whatever the reason, whenever the time, whether it's me, or any one of you, we all seek to understand the depth of the question, *"Why Don't You Like Me?"*

Appendix A—Glossary of Diversity, Equity, and Inclusion Terms

These definitions are provided from multiple sources, although these two were primary:

- The American Society for Engineering Education (ASEE), Committee for Diversity, Equity and Inclusion (CDEI), Annual Conference 2019, Tampa, Florida
- Breaking Through Bias (Kramer and Harris)

ABLEISM	The system of oppression based on ability; assumes disabled people as flawed, insufficient, and inferior. Includes assumptions about what is 'normal' and results in the marginalization of the disabled. In brief, it is the unearned privilege afforded to non-disabled people.
AGENTIC	Derived from the word 'agency.' A person with agentic characteristics exhibits stereotypically masculine traits, such as being aggressive, assertive, competitive, independent, and self-confident. Agentic also refers to being proactive, strong, forceful, loud, stable, unemotional, and a risk-taker.
ASEXUAL	An adjective used to describe people who do not experience sexual attraction (e.g., asexual person).
ASSET PERSPECTIVE	Students' cultural differences are seen as beneficial to the learning environment, as opposed to a deficit perspective, where cultural differences are perceived as detrimental to the learning environment.

ATTUNED GENDER COMMUNICATION	Refers to an integrative series of steps to avoid or overcome career biases women face because of the gender stereotypes operating in the workplace.
BACKLASH	A catchall term referring to the negative consequences women often experience when they act in agentic ways.
BENEVOLENT BIAS	An attitude often expressed by senior men believing traditional gender stereotypes correctly characterize women's capacities and appropriate roles.
BIAS	A generally unconscious attitude that people in one stereotype classification are better or preferable to people in another stereotype classification.
BISEXUAL	A person who has significant romantic, emotional, physical, and/or sexual attractions to both men and women, but not necessarily simultaneously or equally. Included in the LGBTQ acronym.

CISGENDER	Denoting or relating to a person whose sense of personal identity and gender corresponds with their birth sex.
CODE SWITCHING	The practice of shifting the language you use or the way you express yourself in your conversations and environment. Decoding is the awareness and deciphering of different cultural codes. Read the NPR article "Five Reasons Why People Code-Switch" to learn more about this practice.
COMMUNAL	Derived from 'community. A person with communal characteristics exhibits stereotypically feminine traits, such as being nurturing, kind, sympathetic, concerned with the needs of others, socially sensitive, warm, approachable, and understanding. This person tends to be solicitous of others' feelings and is concerned about maintaining cordial relationships, as well as emotional, sentimental, gentle, modest, and friendly.

CULTURE	Implies the integrated patterns of human behavior, including thoughts, communications, actions, customs, beliefs, values, and institutions of racial, ethnic, religious, or social groups.
CULTURAL CAPITAL	The accumulation of knowledge, behaviors, and skills (education, intellect, style of speech, style of dress, etc.) promoting social mobility in a stratified society. Cultural capital provides social advantage and power to individuals whose cultures reflect dominant social norms.
CULTURAL COMPETENCE	The ability to understand one's own—and others'—cultural backgrounds and values; to be aware of how different cultural backgrounds create different perspectives (Gay, 2002; Harrison et al., 2010) and to use knowledge and strategies to allow the culturally-diverse to successfully learn and work together (Cross et al., 1989).

CULTURAL MISMATCH	Occurs when gaps exist between students and educators regarding their racial, cultural, ethnic, social, and linguistic identities. Often times these gaps lead to misunderstandings that harm students.
CULTURALLY RESPONSIVE TEACHING	CRT is a teaching style where educators learn the cultural backgrounds, lived experiences, and learning styles of their students to better reach and teach them. In CRT, educators bring student identities to the center. (Geneva Gay)
CULTURAL STEREOTYPE	Beliefs (within one's culture), leading to assumptions about characteristics, behaviors, and social norms. "The problem with stereotypes is not that they are untrue, but that they are incomplete. They make one story become the only story." Chimamanda Ngozi Adichie, "The Danger of the Single Story," TED Talk

DISABILITY

Depending on the model informing the definition, (i.e., medical, social, economic, feminist, legal, social justice, etc.), social, historical, political, and mythological coordinates impact the actual meaning of disability and disabled people as objects of institutional discourse.

DOUBLE BIND

A situation in which a woman suffers adverse career consequences whichever way she behaves: if she is communal, she is likable, but not regarded as a leader; if she is agentic, she is competent but regarded as not as likable and subject to backlash.

EDUCATIONAL EQUITY

Refers to the principle of fairness in education. While it is often used interchangeably with the related principle of equality, equity encompasses a wide variety of educational models, programs, and strategies that may be considered fair, but are not necessarily equal. Equity is giving every student what they need to succeed, as opposed to giving every student the same.

FEMININE STEREOTYPES	The traditional, often unconscious beliefs that women are and should be communal and should not be (very) agentic.
FOOD INSECURITY	Food insecurity is the state of being without reliable access to a sufficient quantity of affordable, nutritious food. In 2017, an estimated 1 in 8 Americans were food insecure, equating to 40 million Americans (including more than 12 million children).
FUNDS OF KNOWLEDGE	Refers to the knowledge developed from one's home culture. The term originates from Luis Moll, who defines it as "…historically accumulated and culturally developed bodies of knowledge and skills essential for household or individual functioning and well-being." (Moll et al., 1992, p. 133).

GAY	A term used to describe an individual who is emotionally, physically, and/or sexually attracted to members of the same sex. This term is usually used in relation to men but can describe anyone who does not identify as heterosexual or straight. Included in the LGBTQ acronym.
GENDER	A socially constructed system of classification ascribing qualities of masculinity and femininity to people.
GENDER IDENTITY	A person's internal sense of themselves as a specific gender.
GENDER EXPRESSION/ IMAGE/DISPLAY	The external presentation of self as gendered through cultural identifiers/ markers such as clothing, behaviors, etc.
IMPRESSION MANAGEMENT	A person's conscious efforts to behave and communicate in ways designed to shape or change the impressions other people have of him or her.

GENDER-QUEER	A self-identifying term for someone who rejects the male/female gender binary in favor of a more fluid, nontraditional identity that merges or blurs characteristics of gender and gender norms.
HETEROSEXISM	The system of oppression which assumes heterosexuality as the norm, favors heterosexuals, and denigrates and stigmatizes anyone whose gender or sexual behavior is considered non-heterosexual.
HUMANIZING PEDAGOGY	According to Salazar (2013), a 'humanizing pedagogy' is additive, as opposed to focusing on deficits; it utilizes students' prior knowledge and connects it to new learning, thereby legitimizing students' home languages and cultures. In such pedagogy, students are viewed as experts.

IMPLICIT BIAS   The attitudes or stereotypes affecting understanding, actions, or decisions in an unconscious manner. These are often unrecognized and may not align with one's declared beliefs and values. Visit implicit.harvard.edu to take the Implicit Association Test (IAT) and discover your implicit biases. Awareness is the first step!

INTERSECTIONALITY   An approach—largely advanced by women of color—arguing that classifications such as gender, race, class, and others cannot be examined in isolation from one another; they interact and intersect in individuals' lives, in society, in social systems, and are mutually constitutive. The interconnected nature of social categorizations can create overlapping and interdependent systems of discrimination or advantage.

INTERSEX	An umbrella term describing people born with reproductive or sexual anatomy and/or a chromosome pattern that can't be classified as typically male or female. Avoid the outdated and derogatory term 'hermaphrodite.'
LATINX	(Pronounced La-TEEN-ex) A non-gender-specific way of referring to people of Latin American descent. Other ways of referring to people of Latin American descent are Latinos, Latina, Latin@, Latino. The 'x' replaces 'o' and 'a,' which are gendered suffixes. It moves beyond terms like Latino/a & Latin@, which still reinforce a gender binary.
LESBIAN	A term used to describe a woman whose primary romantic, emotional, physical, and sexual attractions are to other women. Included in the LGBTQ acronym.

LGBT, LGBTQ+, AND LGBTQIA

Umbrella terms referring to the community as a whole. The letters stand for Lesbian, Gay, Bisexual, Transgender, Queer, Questioning, intersex, Asexual, and Allied (see separate definitions for these words).

MARGINALIZATION

The treatment of a person, group, or concept as insignificant or peripheral. Marginalized people, for example, are consistently confined to the lower or peripheral edges of society or groups because they are commonly seen as different from perceived norms and dominant cultures. They often experience disadvantage and discrimination stemming from systemic social inequalities and injustices. However, unintentional micro-inequities in interpersonal relationships can also cause marginalization. For example, women and people of color are marginalized in STEM careers, and, as a result, underrepresented.

MASCULINE STEREOTYPE	The traditional, often unconscious assumption that men are and should be agentic, and they should not need to be (very) communal.
MICRO-AGGRESSIONS	A type of micro-message. See Micro-messages.
MICRO-MESSAGES	Small, subtle, unconscious messages sent and received when communicating with others. Micro-messages can be either positive microaffirmations or negative micro-inequities that communicate value to an individual. Micro-messages relay through words and nonverbal communication, contextual cues in the classroom and school, and written feedback.
MIND PRIMING	A technique for conditioning or focusing your mind, so you behave in more positive, forceful, and confident ways.

MULTICULTURAL EDUCATION	Considers acknowledging, recognizing, and incorporating diverse cultures into institutions on a large scale. Nieto (1996) defines it as "...a process of comprehensive school reform and basic education for all students...Multicultural education permeates the curriculum and instructional strategies used in schools, as well as the interactions among teachers, students, and parents, and the very way that schools conceptualize the nature of teaching and learning." (p. 307). Although multicultural education is similar to CRT, CRT focuses more narrowly on how educators can acknowledge and utilize the diverse cultures of their students in their practice.
PANSEXUAL	The sexual, romantic, or emotional attraction towards people regardless of their sex or gender identity. Pansexuality rejects the gender binary.
PEOPLE FIRST LANGUAGE (PFL)	Puts the person before the disability. 'People with disabilities' acknowledges that individuals with disabilities are people first and not their diagnosis or disability.

PERSON OF COLOR
An individual who is not white or of European parentage. It is best to use the phrasing 'people of color,' 'students of color,' 'communities of color,' etc. instead of terms like 'racial minorities' or 'nonwhite' when describing people. The latter terms are white-centric and marginalize people of color. When possible, it is better to specifically identify people based on their race or ethnicity, such as American Indian, Alaskan Native, Asian, black, African American, Hispanic, Latino/a, Native Hawaiian, Pacific Islander, or white, recognizing that many people hold multiple racial identities. It is also important to note: not all black people in the U.S. are or identify as African Americans. The racial identity of black immigrant groups, such as Africans or Afro-Caribbeans, can vary. Learn more: The Journey From 'Colored' To 'Minorities' To 'People of Color' (NPR) n.pr/1dVfc6b; The Changing Definition of African-American (Smithsonian).

POWER POSING	A technique for using your body posture to positively affect your self-image. Posing in a high-power position for two minutes, such as the Wonder Woman position or the runner's victory stance) increases your testosterone and reduces your cortisol, thereby improving your confidence and reducing your anxiety.
QUEER	A term people often use to express fluid identities and orientations. Often used interchangeably with 'LGBTQ.' Included in the LGBTQ acronym. The Q in LGBTQ can also stand for Questioning.
RACE	A social construct dividing people into groups based on factors such as physical appearance, ancestry, culture, history, etc., a social, historical, and political classification system.

RACISM

A system of oppression involving systematic subordination of members of targeted racial groups by those who have relatively more social power. This subordination occurs at the individual, cultural, and institutional levels.

RESTORATIVE
JUSTICE

A theory of justice emphasizing repairing the harm caused by criminal behavior. It is best accomplished through cooperative processes that include all stakeholders. This can add to the transformation of people, relationships, and communities.

SAFE ZONE

A place marked with a logo to indicate it is a safe place for marginalized students (particularly the LGBTQ+ community), where they will be listened to, supported, and understood.

SELF-EFFICACY   One's belief they can be successful in a specific task or challenge and answers the question: "Can I do this?" An individual with high self-efficacy is more likely to adopt and commit to more challenging goals, and an individual with low self-efficacy is more likely to avoid challenges.

SELF-MONITORING   A state of the acute self-awareness of the impressions you are making on the people with whom you are dealing. This awareness allows you to modify your behavior and communication and to make the impression needed in the situation.

SOCIAL CAPITAL   The networks of relationships among people who live and work in a particular society, enabling the society to function effectively. Social capital includes the resources inherent in social relations such as trust, norms, reciprocity, and knowledge from exposure to certain experiences.

SOCIAL CLASS	People's socioeconomic status (upper class, middle class, lower class, working-class). Based on factors such as wealth, occupation, education, income, etc.
STEREOTYPES	Unconscious mental mechanisms we use to classify people and then ascribe characteristics to all members of these classes. The characteristics ascribed have no basis or validity in reality.
STEREOTYPE THREAT	A socially premised psychological threat arising when one is in a situation or doing something for which a negative stereotype about one's group applies (Steele & Aronson, 1995). Awareness of negative stereotypes negatively impacts the performance of members of marginalized groups in certain situations.

TRANSGENDER	An umbrella term for people whose gender identity and/or expression is different from cultural expectations based on the sex they were assigned at birth. Being transgender does not imply any specific sexual orientation. Therefore, transgender people may identify as straight, gay, lesbian, bisexual, etc. Included in the LGBTQ acronym.
UNIVERSAL DESIGN	The design of products and environments to be usable by all people, to the greatest extent possible, without the need for adaptation or specialized design.
WHITE PRIVILEGE	Institutional set of benefits, including greater access to resources and power, bestowed upon people classified as white.
WHITE SUPREMACY	The assumption or theory that whites are superior to all other races and should be in power and control. It is a structural system built into the founding of our nation, our culture, and our institutions and is still in place today.

According to the American Society for Engineering Education (ASEE), Committee for Diversity, Equity and Inclusion (CDEI), their definitions in this appendix are derived from multiple resources including:

- Eliminating Barriers through Culturally Responsive Teaching (see page 78-81) https:// www.napequity.org/product/ crt-toolkit /
- White Privilege Conference (see page 10-11): http:/ /bit.ly/ WPC2017defs
- ASU—Intergroup Relations Center Glossary: https://www. asu.edu/ provost/Backup/intergroup/ resources/glossary.pdf

Appendix A.1—Citations

Cross, T. L., Bazron, B. J., Dennis, K. W., & Isaacs, M. R. (1989). Towards a Culturally Competent System of Care: A Monograph on Effective Services for Minority Children Who Are Severely Emotionally Disturbed.

Gay, G. (2002). Preparing for culturally responsive teaching. Journal of Teacher Education, 53(2), 106-116.

Harrison, L., Carson, R. L., & Burden, J. (2010). Physical Education Teachers' Cultural Competency. Journal of Teaching in Physical Education, 29(2)184-198.

Moll, L. C., Amanti, C., Neff, D., & Gonzalez, N. (1992). Funds of knowledge for teaching: Using a qualitative approach to connect homes and classrooms. Theory Into Practice, 31(2), 132-141.

Nieto, S. (1996). Affirming diversity: the sociopolitical context of multicultural education (2nd ed.). White Plains, N.Y: Longman Publishers USA.

Steele, C. M., & Aronson, J. (1995). Stereotype Threat and the Intellectual Test Performance of African Americans. Journal of Personality and Social Psychology, 69(5), 797-811.

Bibliography

The work in this book is the result of hundreds of articles and books. These highlights are the most prevalent and applicable to the date of this publication.

Abrams, D. (2011). *Man down: Proof beyond a reasonable doubt that women are better cops, drivers, gamblers, spies, world leaders, beer tasters, hedge fund managers, and just about everything else.* New York: Abrams.

Alsop, R. (2008). *The trophy kids grow up: How the Millennial Generation is shaking up the workplace.* San Francisco: Jossey-Bass.

Allen, I., & Seaman, J (2017). Digital Learning Compass: Distance Education Enrollment Report 2017. Babson Survey Research Group.

Annis, B. & Nesbitt, R. (2017). Results at the Top: Using Gender Intelligence to Create Breakthrough Growth. Hoboken, N.J., John Wiley & Sons, Inc.

American Psychological Association (APA), (2018). Stress in America: Generation Z. Stress in America Survey.

Banaji, M. & Greenwald, A. (2016). Blind Spot: Hidden Biases of Good People. New York, N.Y., Bantam.

Bargh, J. (2017). *Before You Know It.* New York, N.Y., Simon & Schuster.

Blumenstyk, G. (2018). *The Adult Student.* The Chronicle of Higher Education.

Carlson, S. (2018). Sustaining the College Business Model. The Chronicle of Higher Education.

Cellini, S. (2018). Gainfully Employed? New Evidence on the Earnings, Employment and Debt of For-Profit Certificate Students. Brookings Institute. Retrieved from https://www.brookings.edu/blog/brown-center-chalkboard/2018/02/09/gainfully-employed-new-evidence-on-the-earnings-employment-and-debt-of-for-profit-certificate-students/

Dimock, M. (2019). Defining Generations: Where Millennials End and Generation Z Begins. Pew Research Center. January 17, 2019.

DOJ (2018). Hate Crime Statistics 2017. Department of Justice, Federal Bureau of Investigations. Downloaded from https://ucr.fbi.gov/hate-crime/2017.

Fortin, P. (2018). How to Fix the Adjunct Crisis. The Chronicle of Higher Education. Downloaded from the internet May 31, 2018. https://www.chronicle.com/article/How-to-Fix-the-Adjunct-Crisis/243535.

Frey, W. (2018). The Millennial Generation: A Demographic Bridge to America's Diverse Future. *Metropolitan Policy Program at Brookings*. Downloaded January 2, 2018 from https://www.brookings.edu/research/millennials/.

Frey, W. (2018). Diversity Explosion: How New Racial Demographics Are Remaking America. Washington, D.C., The Brookings Institution.

Fry, R. (2018). *More Adults Now Share Their Living Space, Driven in Part by Parents Living with Their Adult Children.* Pew Research Center. January 31. Retrieved from http://www.pewresearch.org/fact-tank/2018/01/31/more-adults-now-share-their-living-space-driven-in-part-by-parents-living-with-their-adult-children/

Geiger, A. & Bialik, K. (2019). The Changing Face of Congress in 6 Charts. Pew Research Center. February 15, 2019.

House, J. (2018). *Report: For Many Adult Learners, Going to College is Desirable but Unaffordable.* Education Dive. Retrieved from https://www.educationdive.com/news/report-for-many-adult-learners-going-to-college-is-desirable-but-unafford/514902/

Kramer, A., & Harris, A. (2016). Breaking Through Bias: Communication techniques for Women to Succeed at Work. New York, NY: Bibliomotion, Inc.

Lipman, J. (2018). That's What She Said. New York, N.Y., Harper Collins Publishers.

National Science Foundation (NSF). (2016). *Science and engineering indicators 2016*. Arlington, VA: National Science Foundation.

Panetta, G. & Lee, S. (2019). Meet the 116th Congress. Business Insider, Jan. 5, 2019. Downloaded from https://www.businessinsider.com/changes-in-gender-racial-diversity-between-the-115th-and-116th-house-2018-12.

Parker, K, Graf, N. & Igielnik, R. (2019). Generation Z Looks a Lot Like Millennials on Key Social and Political Issues. Pew Research Center. January 17, 2019.

PEW Research Center (2018). U.S. Immigration—Lessons 1-5. Pew Research Center.

Ratanjee, V. & Green, A. (2018). How to Reduce Bias in Your Succession and Promotion Plans. Gallup, Inc. Downloaded from https://news.gallup.com/businessjournal/235436/poll/232319/facebook-users-privacy-concerns-2011.aspx.

Saeed, J. (2018). 3 Enrollment Pressures to Prepare for in 2018. Education Advisory Board (EAB). Retrieved from https://www.eab.com/research-and-insights/academic-affairs-forum/expert-insights/2018/2018-challenges-for-academic-affairs.

Seemiller, C. & Grace, M. (2016). *Generation Z Goes to College*. San Francisco, CA.: Jossey-Bass.

Selingo, J. (2016). *2026 the Decade Ahead—The Seismic Shifts Transforming the Future of Higher Education.* The Chronicle of Higher Education, Inc.

Selingo, J. (2017). *2026 The Decade Ahead: The Seismic Shifts Transforming the Future of Higher Education.* The Chronicle of Higher Education Report.

Scott, M. & Nightingale, D. (2018). The Education-Jobs "Mix-Match": How Much Opportunity is There for the College-Educated Workforce in America's Metropolitan Areas? Urban Institute. Washington, D.C.

Springer, M. (2019). Project and Program Management: A Competency-Based Approach. 4th ed. West Lafayette, IN: Purdue University Press.

Stone, L. (2018). The Decline of American Fertility. *Fortune Magazine.* February 1, 2018. P. 16.

Student Loan Hero. (2018). A Look at the Shocking Student Loan Debt Statistics for 2018. Student Loan Hero. Downloaded from https://studentloanhero.com/student-loan-debt-statistics/.

Twenge, J. (2017). *iGen.* New York, N.Y.: Simon and Schuster Inc.

U.S. Census Bureau (2018). Older People Projected to Outnumber Children for First Time in U.S. History. United States Census Bureau, March 13, 2018. Release Number CB18-41.

Vespa, J., Armstrong, D., and Medina, L. (2018). Demographic Turning Points for the United States: Population Projections for 2020 to 2060. Current population Reports, P25-1144, U.S. Census Bureau, Washington, DC.

About the Author

DR. MITCHELL L. SPRINGER, PMP, SPHR, SHRM-SCP

Dr. Mitchell L. Springer currently serves as an Executive Director for Purdue University's Polytechnic Institute located in West Lafayette, Indiana. He has over thirty-five years of theoretical and defense industry-based practical experience from four disciplines: software engineering, systems engineering, program management, and human resources.

Dr. Springer possesses a significant strength in pattern recognition, analyzing, and improving organizational systems. He is internationally recognized and has contributed to scholarship more than 300 books, articles, presentations, editorials, and reviews on software development methodologies, management, organizational change, and program management.

Mitchell Springer sits on many university and community boards and advisory committees. He is the recipient of numerous awards and recognitions, including local, regional and national recognition for leadership in diversity, equity, and inclusion.

Dr. Springer is the President of the Indiana Council for Continuing Education as well as the Past-Chair of the Continuing Professional Development Division of the American Society for Engineering Education (ASEE). Dr. Springer serves as a Division Delegate to the ASEE Committee on Diversity, Equity, and Inclusion.

He received his Bachelor of Science degree in Computer Science from Purdue University and his MBA and doctorate in Adult and Community Education with a Cognate in Executive Development from Ball State University. Dr. Springer's certifications include Project Management Professional (PMP), Senior Professional in Human Resources (SPHR & SHRM-SCP) in Alternate Dispute Resolution (ADR), and in civil and domestic mediation.

Dr. Springer is a State of Indiana Registered domestic mediator.

9 781946 533388